Cram101 Textbook Outlines to accompany:

Palestine and the Arab-Israeli Conflict

Charles D. Smith, 6th Edition

A Content Technologies Inc. publication (c) 2012.

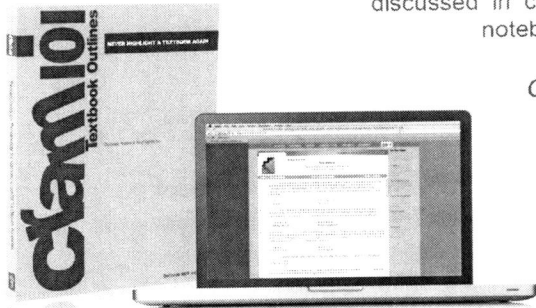

Learning System

Cram101 Textbook Outlines is a learning system. The notes in this book are the highlights of your textbook, you will never have to highlight a book again.

How to use this book. Take this book to class, it is your notebook for the lecture. The notes and highlights on the left hand side of the pages follow the outline and order of the textbook. All you have to do is follow along while your instructor presents the lecture. Circle the items emphasized in class and add other important information on the right side. With Cram101 Textbook Outlines you'll spend less time writing and more time listening. Learning becomes more efficient.

Cram101.com Online

Increase your studying efficiency by using Cram101.com's practice tests and online reference material. It is the perfect complement to Cram101 Textbook Outlines. Use self-teaching matching tests or simulate in-class testing with comprehensive multiple choice tests, or simply use Cram's true and false tests for quick review. Cram101.com even allows you to enter your in-class notes for an integrated studying format combining the textbook notes with your class notes.

Visit **www.Cram101.com**, click Sign Up at the top of the screen, and enter **DK73DW7826** in the promo code box on the registration screen. Your access to www.Cram101.com is discounted by 50% because you have purchased this book. Sign up and stop highlighting textbooks forever.

Palestine and the Arab-Israeli Conflict
Charles D. Smith, 6th

CONTENTS

Chapter 1. THE MIDDLE EAST AND PALESTINE TO 1914: An Overview

Christianity	Christianity is a monotheistic religion based on the life and teachings of Jesus as presented in canonical gospels and other New Testament writings. Adherents of the Christian faith are known as Christians. Mainstream Christianity teaches that the Greatest commandment is love or Agape.
Egypt	The Roman province of Egypt was established in 30 BC after Octavian (the future emperor Augustus) defeated his rival Mark Antony, deposed his lover Queen Cleopatra VII and annexed the Ptolemaic kingdom of Egypt to the Roman Empire. The province encompassed most of modern-day Egypt except for the Sinai Peninsula (which would later be conquered by Trajan). Aegyptus was bordered by the provinces of Creta et Cyrenaica to the West and Judaea to the East.
Henry	Henry is an English male given name and a surname, from the Old French Henry derived itself from the Germanic name Haimric, which was derived from the word elements haim, meaning "home" and ric, meaning "power, ruler". Harry, its English short form, was considered the "spoken form" of Henry in medieval England. Most English kings named Henry were called Harry.
Jerusalem	Jerusalem [ii] is the capital of Israel, though not internationally recognized as such.[iii] If the area and population of East Jerusalem is included, it is Israel's largest city in both population and area, with a population of 763,800 residents over an area of 125.1 km^2 (48.3 sq mi).[iv] Located in the Judean Mountains, between the Mediterranean Sea and the northern edge of the Dead Sea, modern Jerusalem has grown far beyond the boundaries of the Old City. Jerusalem is a holy city to the three major Abrahamic religions--Judaism, Christianity and Islam. In Judaism, Jerusalem has been the holiest city since, according to the Torah, King David of Israel first established it as the capital of the united Kingdom of Israel in c. 1000 BCE, and his son Solomon commissioned the building of the First Temple in the city.
Judea	35°18′23″E? / ?31.69889°N 35.30639°E

Chapter 1. THE MIDDLE EAST AND PALESTINE TO 1914: An Overview

---

Judea, when Roman Judea was renamed Syria Palaestina following the Jewish Bar Kokhba revolt.

Etymology

The name Judea is a Greek and Roman adaptation of the name "Judah", which originally encompassed the territory of the Israelite tribe of that name and later of the ancient Kingdom of Judah. It was the name in use in English throughout history until the Jordanian occupation of the area.

Lebanon	Lebanon is a mural size painting by Nabil Kanso depicting the Lebanese Civil War in a scene invoking the spirit and character of the people in the midst of horror and violence gripping the country. Amid the scene of chaos and devastation, two central figures reach across toward each other symbolically to represent the appeal for unity in defiance of the forces of division, destruction, and terror.

Description

Painted in oil on linen and completed in 1983, the painting Lebanon measures 28 feet (8.5 meters) long by 10 feet (3meters) tall.

Muhammad	Muhammad ibn 'Abdullah (ca. 570/571 - June 8, 632), (Monday, 12th Rabi' al-Awwal, Year 11 A.H). is considered the founder of the religion of Islam, and is regarded by Muslims as a messenger and prophet of God, the last law-bearer in a series of Islamic prophets, and, by most Muslims, the last prophet of Islam as taught by the Qur'an. Muslims thus consider him the restorer of an uncorrupted original monotheistic faith (islam) of Adam, Noah, Abraham, Moses, Jesus and other prophets.
Palestine	Palestine (Greek: Παλαιστ?νη, Palaistine; Latin: Palaestina; Hebrew: ????????? Eretz-Yisra'el, (formerly also ????????, Palestina); Arabic: ??????? Filas?in, Falas?in, Filis?in) is a conventional name used, among others, to describe a geographic region between the Mediterranean Sea and the Jordan River, and various adjoining lands.

Chapter 1. THE MIDDLE EAST AND PALESTINE TO 1914: An Overview

	Other terms for the same area include Canaan, Zion, the Land of Israel, and the Holy Land. Southern Levant is another purely geographic term, often implemented for the region, which does not have political or theologic implications.
Philistines	The Philistines were a people who occupied the southern coast of Canaan, their territory being named Philistia in later contexts. It is theorized that the latter Philistines originated among the "sea peoples". Modern archaeology has also suggested early cultural links with the Mycenean world in Greece.
Samaria	Samaria is a term used for a mountainous region roughly corresponding to the northern part of the West Bank. According to 1 Kings 16:24, it is derived from the individual [or clan] Shemer, from whom Omri purchased the site. The name was the only name used for this area from ancient times until the Jordanian conquest of 1948, at which point the Jordanian occupiers coined the term West Bank.
Syria	Syria, officially the Syrian Arab Republic, is a country in Western Asia, bordering Lebanon and the Mediterranean Sea to the West, Turkey to the north, Iraq to the east, Jordan to the south, and Israel to the southwest.
	The name Syria formerly comprised the entire region of the Levant, while the modern state encompasses the site of several ancient kingdoms and empires, including the Eblan civilization of the third millennium BC. In the Islamic era, its capital city, Damascus, was the seat of the Umayyad Empire and a provincial capital of the Mamluk Empire. Damascus is one of the oldest continuously inhabited cities in the world.
Temple	In the Latter Day Saint movement, a temple is a building dedicated to be a house of God and is reserved for special forms of worship. A temple differs from a church meetinghouse, which is used for weekly worship services. Temples have been a significant part of the Latter Day Saint movement since early in its inception.
Temple Mount	The Temple Mount, also known in the Bible as Mount Moriah (some also identify it with the biblical Mount Zion) and by Muslims as the Noble Sanctuary (Bait-ul-Muqaddas), is a religious site in the Old City of Jerusalem.

Chapter 1. THE MIDDLE EAST AND PALESTINE TO 1914: An Overview

Judaism regards the Temple Mount as the place where God chose the Divine Presence to rest (Isa 8:18); it was from here the world expanded into its present form and where God gathered the dust used to create the first man, Adam.{According to the sages of the Talmud[13]} The site is the location of Abraham's binding of Isaac, and of two Jewish Temples. According to the Bible the site should function as the center of all national life - government, judicial and, of course, religious center (Deut 12:5-26; 14:23-25; 15:20; 16:2-16; 17:8-10; 26: 2; 31: 11; Isa 2: 2-5; Oba 1:21; Psa 48) .

West Bank

The West Bank of the Jordan River is the landlocked geographical eastern part of the Palestinian territories located in the Western Asia. To the west, north, and south, the West Bank shares borders with the state of Israel. To the east, across the Jordan River, lies the Hashemite Kingdom of Jordan.

Zionism

Zionism is a Jewish political movement that, in its broadest sense, has supported the self-determination of the Jewish people in a sovereign Jewish national homeland. Since the establishment of the State of Israel, the Zionist movement continues primarily to advocate on behalf of the Jewish state and address threats to its continued existence and security. In a less common usage, the term may also refer to 1) non-political, Cultural Zionism, founded and represented most prominently by Ahad Ha'am; and 2) political support for the State of Israel by non-Jews, as in Christian Zionism.

Ancients

The Ancients were a group of English artists who were brought together by their attraction to archaism in art and admiration for the work of William Blake. The core members of the Ancients were Samuel Palmer, George Richmond, Edward Calvert. They met in Blake's apartment, dubbed the "House of Interpreter" and at the home of Samuel Palmer in the Kent village of Shoreham.

Assassination

An assassination is "to murder (a usually prominent person) by a sudden and/or secret attack, often for political reasons." An additional definition is "the act of deliberately killing someone especially a public figure, usually for hire or for political reasons."

Chapter 1. THE MIDDLE EAST AND PALESTINE TO 1914: An Overview

Assassinations may be prompted by religious, ideological, political, or military motives. Additionally, assassins may be prompted by financial gain, revenge for perceived grievances, a desire to acquire fame or notoriety (that is, a psychological need to garner personal public recognition), a wish to form some kind of "relationship" with the public figure, a wish or at least willingness to be killed or commit suicide in the attack.

Etymology

The word assassin is derived from the word Hashshashin, and shares its etymological roots with hashish .

Prophet

In religion, a prophet is an individual who is claimed to have been contacted by the supernatural or the divine, and serves as an intermediary with humanity, delivering this newfound knowledge from the supernatural entity to other people. The message that the prophet conveys is called a prophecy.

Claims of prophets have existed in many cultures through history, including Judaism, Christianity, Islam, the Sybilline and the Pythia, known as the Oracle of Delphi, in Ancient Greece, Zoroaster, the Völuspá in Old Norse and many others.

Response

A response is the second half of one of a set of preces, the said or sung answer by the congregation or choir to a versicle said or sung by an officiant or cantor. In the following opening of the Anglican service of Evening Prayer according to the Book of Common Prayer (BCP), the first line is the versicle and the second is the response.

In some liturgical books (such as hymnals or breviaries) the symbol "R/" or "?" is used to denote a response.

Aqaba

Aqaba is a coastal town in the far south of Jordan. It is the capital of Aqaba Governorate. Aqaba is strategically important to Jordan as it is the country's only seaport.

Chapter 1. THE MIDDLE EAST AND PALESTINE TO 1914: An Overview

Barak	Barak, Al-Buraq the son of Abinoam from Kedesh in Naphtali, was a military general in the Book of Judges in the Bible. He was the commander of the army of Deborah, the prophetess and heroine of the Hebrew Bible. Barak and Deborah are credited with defeating the Canaanite armies led by Sisera, who for twenty years had oppressed the Israelites.
Cold War	Cold War is a video game developed by Czech developer Mindware Studios and published by DreamCatcher Games (Linux Game Publishing for Linux). The game is similar to the Splinter Cell series of games in that it uses a stealth-action system of gameplay. The game distinguishes itself by adding an invention system where the player can use seemingly useless objects to create tools and weapons.
Ehud	Ehud ben-Gera is described in the Biblical Book of Judges as a judge who was sent by God to deliver the Israelites from the Moabite yoke. Ehud was sent to the Moabite King Eglon on the pretext of delivering the Israelites' annual tribute. He had blacksmiths make a double-edged shortsword about eighteen inches long, useful for a stabbing thrust.
Labor Zionism	Labor Zionism can be described as the major stream of the left wing of the Zionist movement. It was, for many years, the most significant tendency among Zionists and Zionist organizational structure. It saw itself as the Zionist sector of the historic Jewish labor movements of Eastern and Central Europe, eventually developing local units in most countries with sizeable Jewish populations.
Libya	Libya was a satrapy of the Achaemenid Empire according to King Darius I of Persia Naqshe Rustam and King Xerxes I of Persia' Daiva inscription. It is also mentioned as being part of the 6th district by Herodotus, which also included Cyrene, a Greek colony in Libya. When King Cambyses II of Persia conquered Egypt, the king of Cyrene, Arcesilaus III, sided with Persia.

Chapter 1. THE MIDDLE EAST AND PALESTINE TO 1914: An Overview

Orthodox	Orthodox Basketball Club formerly known as Fastlink Basketball Club is a Jordanian basketball club based in Amman, Jordan. They compete in the Jordanian Basketball Federation. Tournament records WABA Champions Cup • 1999: Champions • 2001: 2nd place • 2002: 2nd place • 2004: 1st place • 2008: 2nd place • 2009: 1st place Asia Champions Cup • 1988: 5th place • 1996: 7th place • 1999: 6th place .
Revisionist Zionism	Revisionist Zionism is a nationalist faction within the Zionist movement. It is the founding ideology of the non-religious right in Israel, and was the chief ideological competitor to the dominant socialist Labor Zionism. Revisionism is represented primarily by the Likud Party.
Sharm el-Sheikh	Sharm el-Sheikh is a city situated on the southern tip of the Sinai Peninsula, in South Sinai Governorate, Egypt, on the coastal strip along the Red Sea with a population of approximately 35,000 (2008). Sharm el-Sheikh is the administrative hub of Egypt's South Sinai Governorate which includes the smaller coastal towns of Dahab and Nuweiba as well as the mountainous interior, Saint Catherine's Monastery and Mount Sinai. Name Sharm el-Sheikh is sometimes called the "City of Peace", referring to the large number of international peace conferences that have been held there.

Chapter 1. THE MIDDLE EAST AND PALESTINE TO 1914: An Overview

Politics	Aristotle's Politics is a work of political philosophy. The end of the Nicomachean Ethics declared that the inquiry into ethics necessarily follows into politics, and the two works are frequently considered to be parts of a larger treatise, or perhaps connected lectures, dealing with the "philosophy of human affairs." The title of the Politics literally means "the things concerning the polis." Composition The literary character of the Politics is subject to some dispute, growing out of the textual difficulties that attended the loss of Aristotle's works. Book III ends with a sentence that is repeated almost verbatim at the start of Book VII, while the intervening Books IV-VI seem to have a very different flavor from the rest; Book IV seems to refer several times back to the discussion of the best regime contained in Books VII-VIII. Some editors have therefore inserted Books VII-VIII after Book III. At the same time, however, references to the "discourses on politics" that occur in the Nicomachean Ethics suggest that the treatise as a whole ought to conclude with the discussion of education that occurs in Book VIII of the Politics, although it is not certain that Aristotle is referring to the Politics here.
Damascus	Damascus is the capital and the second largest city of Syria as well as one of the country's 14 governorates. The Damascus Governorate is ruled by a governor appointed by the Minister of Interior. In addition to being the oldest continuously inhabited city in the world, Damascus is a major cultural and religious center of the Levant.
Ariel	Ariel is an Israeli settlement and a city in the central West Bank. Established in 1978, its population at the end of 2009 was 17,600, including 7,000 immigrants who came to Israel after 1990. It is the fourth largest Jewish settlement city in the West Bank., after Modi'in Illit, Beitar Illit, and Ma'ale Adumim. In Hebrew, Ariel, literally means 'Lion of God'.

17

Chapter 1. THE MIDDLE EAST AND PALESTINE TO 1914: An Overview

Bar Kokhba revolt	The Bar Kokhba revolt against the Roman Empire was the third major rebellion by the Jews of Judaea Province and the last of the Jewish-Roman Wars. Simon bar Kokhba, the commander of the revolt, was acclaimed as a Messiah, a heroic figure who could restore Israel. The revolt established an independent state of Israel over parts of Judea for over two years, but a Roman army of 12 legions with auxiliaries finally crushed it.
Arabia	Arabia was a satrapy (province) of the Achaemenid Empire and later of the Sassanid Empire, by the name of Arabistan. Achaemenid Era Achaemenid Arabia corresponded to the lands between Egypt and Mesopotamia, known as Arabia Petraea. According to Herodotus, the Cambyses did not subdue the Arabs when he attacked Egypt in 525 BCE. His successor Darius the Great does not mention the Arabs in the Behistun inscription from the first years of his reign, but mentions them in later texts.
Abbasid Caliphate	The Abbasid caliphate, more simply, the Abbasids, was the third of the Islamic caliphates. It was ruled by the Abbasid dynasty of caliphs, who built their capital in Baghdad after overthrowing the Umayyad caliphs from all but the Al Andalus region. The Abbasid caliphate was founded by the descendants of the Islamic prophet Muhammad's youngest uncle, Abbas ibn Abd al-Muttalib, in Harran in 750 CE and shifted its capital in 762 to Baghdad.
Abraham	Abraham, whose birth name was Abram, is the eponymous father of the Abrahamic religions, such as Judaism, Christianity, and Islam, and of the Israelites, Ishmaelites, Edomites, and the Midianites and other peoples, according to both the Hebrew Bible and the Qur'an. He is a descendant of Noah's son Shem. In a contemporary context, Jews are said to be able to trace their ancestry back to Abraham the father of the Hebrew nation, through the line of his second son Isaac.

Chapter 1. THE MIDDLE EAST AND PALESTINE TO 1914: An Overview

Baghdad	Baghdad is the capital of Iraq, as well as the coterminous Baghdad Governorate. With an estimated population between 7 and 7.5 million, it is the largest city in Iraq, the second largest city in the Arab World (after Cairo, Egypt), and the second largest city in Western Asia (after Tehran, Iran).
	Located along the Tigris River, the city was founded in the 8th century and became the capital of the Abbasid Caliphate.
Caliphate	The term caliphate "dominion of a caliph ('successor,')," refers to the first system of government established in Islam, and represented the political unity of the Muslim Ummah (nation). In theory, it is a constitutional republic , meaning that the head of state (the Caliph) and other officials are dicate to the people according to Islamic law, which exercises power over their citizens. It was initially led by Muhammad's disciples as a continuation of the political system the prophet established, known as the 'rashidun caliphates'.
Iraq	Iraq ; officially the Republic of Iraq is a country in Western Asia spanning most of the northwestern end of the Zagros mountain range, the eastern part of the Syrian Desert and the northern part of the Arabian Desert.
	Iraq is bordered by Jordan to the west, Syria to the northwest, Turkey to the north, Iran to the east, and Kuwait and Saudi Arabia to the south. Iraq has a narrow section of coastline measuring 58 km (35 miles) on the northern Persian Gulf.
Christian	A Christian is a person who adheres to Christianity, an Abrahamic, monotheistic religion based on the life and teachings of Jesus of Nazareth as recorded in the Canonical gospels and the letters of the New Testament.
	Central to the Christian faith is love or Agape. Christians also believe Jesus is the Messiah prophesied in the Hebrew Bible, the Son of God, and the savior of mankind from their sins.

Chapter 1. THE MIDDLE EAST AND PALESTINE TO 1914: An Overview

Crusade	Crusade is a Franco-Belgian comics series written by Jean Dufaux, illustrated by Philippe Xavier and published by Le Lombard in French and Cinebook in English.

Story

Volumes

1. Simoun Dja - Nov. 2007 ISBN 978-2-8036-2313-6
2. Le qua'dj - Sept. 2008 ISBN 978-2-8036-2405-8
3. Le maître des machines - May 2009 ISBN 978-2-8036-2536-9
4. Les becs de feu - Nov. 2009 ISBN 978-2-8036-2591-8

Translations

Cinebook Ltd has started publishing Crusade. One album has been released so far:

1. Simoun Dja - May 2008 ISBN 978-1-8491-8061-0
2. Qa'dj - Feb. 2011 ISBN 978-1-8491-8068-9
3. The Master of Machines - July 2011
4. The Fire Beaks - Feb. 2012

.

Dhimmi	A dhimmi, (collectively ??? ????? ahl al-dhimmah, "the people of the dhimma or people of the contract") is a non-Muslim subject of a state governed in accordance with sharia law. The dhimma is a theoretical contract based on a widely held Islamic doctrine granting special status to adherents of Judaism, Christianity, and certain other non-Muslim religions ("People of the Book"). Dhimma provides rights of residence in return for taxes.
Caliph	The Caliph is the head of state in a Caliphate, and the title for the leader of the Islamic Ummah, an Islamic community ruled by the Shari'ah. It is a transcribed version of the Arabic word ????? Khalifah which means "successor" or "representative". Following Muhammad's death in 632, the early leaders of the Muslim nation were called "Khalifat Rasul Allah", the political successors to the messenger of God (referring to Muhammad).

Chapter 1. THE MIDDLE EAST AND PALESTINE TO 1914: An Overview

Catholic	The word catholic comes from the Greek phrase καθ?λου (kath'holou), meaning "on the whole," "according to the whole" or "in general", and is a combination of the Greek words κατ? meaning "about" and ?λος meaning "whole". The word in English can mean either "including a wide variety of things; all-embracing" or "of the Roman Catholic faith." as "relating to the historic doctrine and practice of the Western Church."
	It was first used to describe the Christian Church in the early 2nd century to emphasize its universal scope. In the context of Christian ecclesiology, it has a rich history and several usages.
Ottoman Empire	The Ottoman Empire was an empire that lasted from 27 July 1299 to 29 October 1923.
	At the height of its power, in the 16th and 17th centuries, the empire spanned three continents, controlling much of Southeastern Europe, Western Asia and North Africa. The Ottoman Empire contained 29 provinces and numerous vassal states, some of which were later absorbed into the empire, while others were granted various types of autonomy during the course of centuries. The empire also temporarily gained authority over distant overseas lands through declarations of allegiance to the Ottoman Sultan and Caliph, such as the declaration by the Sultan of Aceh in 1565; or through the temporary acquisitions of islands in the Atlantic Ocean, such as Lanzarote in 1585.
Histories	Histories is a book by Tacitus, written c. 100-110, which covers the Year of Four Emperors following the downfall of Nero, the rise of Vespasian, and the rule of the Flavian Dynasty (69-96) up to the death of Domitian.
	Subject matter
	In one of the first chapters of the Agricola Tacitus said that he wished to speak about the years of Domitian, of Nerva, and of Trajan. In the Historiae the project has been modified: in the introduction, Tacitus says that he will deal with the age of Nerva and Trajan at a later time.

Chapter 1. THE MIDDLE EAST AND PALESTINE TO 1914: An Overview

Aleppo	Aleppo is the largest city in Syria and the capital of Aleppo Governorate, the most populous Syrian governorate. With a population of 2,301,570 (2005 official estimate), it is also the largest city in the Levant. Aleppo is one of the oldest continuously inhabited cities in the world; it has been inhabited since perhaps as early as the 6th millennium BC. Excavations at Tell Qaramel (25 km north of Aleppo) show the area to have been inhabited since the 11th millennium BC, which makes it the oldest known human settlement in the world.
Catholic	The word catholic comes from the Greek phrase καθ?λου (kath'holou), meaning "on the whole," "according to the whole" or "in general", and is a combination of the Greek words κατ? meaning "about" and ?λος meaning "whole". The word in English can mean either "including a wide variety of things; all-embracing" or "of the Roman Catholic faith." as "relating to the historic doctrine and practice of the Western Church." It was first used to describe the Christian Church in the early 2nd century to emphasize its universal scope. In the context of Christian ecclesiology, it has a rich history and several usages.
Druze	The Druze are an esoteric monotheistic religious community found primarily in Syria, Lebanon, Israel, and Jordan, which emerged during the 11th century from Ismailism and incorporated several elements of Gnosticism, Neoplatonism and other philosophies. Some Druze call themselves Ahl al-Tawhid "People of Unitarianism or Monotheism" or al-Muwa??idun "Unitarians, Monotheists." Location The Druze people reside primarily in Syria, Lebanon, and Israel. The Israeli Druze are mostly in Galilee (81%), around Haifa (19%), and in the Golan Heights.

27

Chapter 1. THE MIDDLE EAST AND PALESTINE TO 1914: An Overview

Hebron	Hebron, is located in the southern West Bank, 30 km (19 mi) south of Jerusalem. Nestled in the Judean Mountains, it lies 930 meters (3,050 ft) above sea level. It is the largest city in the West Bank and home to around 165,000 Palestinians, and over 500 Jewish settlers concentrated in and around the old quarter.
Roman Catholic	The term Roman Catholic is generally used on its own to refer to individuals, and in compound forms to refer to worship, parishes, festivals, etc. Its usage has varied, depending on circumstances. It is sometimes identified with one or other of the terms "Catholic", "Western Catholic", and "Roman-Rite Catholic".
Russians	The Russian people are an ethnic group of the East Slavic peoples, primarily living in Russia and neighboring countries. The English term Russians is used to refer to the citizens of Russia, regardless of their ethnicity; the demonym Russian is translated into Russian as rossiyanin, while the ethnic Russians are referred to as russkiye (sg. русский, russkiy).
Alliance	This article incorporates text from Easton's Bible Dictionary (1897), a publication now in the public domain. Abraham formed an alliance with some of the Canaanitish princes (Gen. 14:13), also with Abimelech (21:22-32). Joshua and the elders of Israel entered into an alliance with the Gibeonites (Josh. 9:3-27). When the Israelites entered Canaan they were forbidden to enter into alliances with the inhabitants of the country (Lev. 18:3, 4; 20:22, 23).
Correspondence	In theology, correspondence is the relationship between spiritual and natural realities, or between mental and physical realities. The term was coined by the 18th century theologian Emanuel Swedenborg in his Arcana Coelestia (1749-1756) and Heaven and Hell (1758) and other works. Swedenborg states that there is a correspondence between, for example: thought and speech, between intention and action, between mind and body, and between God and creation.

Chapter 1. THE MIDDLE EAST AND PALESTINE TO 1914: An Overview

Mandate	In Christian theology, a mandate is an order given from God that must be obeyed without question. For example, the mandate given to Abraham to offer his son Isaac as a sacrifice to God. (Genesis 22:1)
Greater Syria	Greater Syria, also known simply as Syria, is a term that denotes a region in the Near East bordering the Eastern Mediterranean Sea or the Levant.

The classical Arabic name for Syria is Sham, which in later ages came to refer only to Damascus in Levantine Arabic, while the pre-Islamic name of the territory, Syria, was used again until the collapse of the Ottoman Empire in 1918.

Historic Syria

The extent of the area known as Syria has changed over time. |

31

Chapter 1. THE MIDDLE EAST AND PALESTINE TO 1914: An Overview

| Ibrahim | Ibrahim is the Arabic name of the prophet Abraham. It is a common first name throughout the Muslim world. |

Given name

- Ibrahim I, Ottoman sultan
- Ibrahim Abatcha, Chadian politician
- Ibrahim Abouleish, Egyptian scientist
- Ibrahim Abu-Lughod, Palestinian academic
- Ibrahim Afellay, Dutch footballer
- Ibrahim Ahmad, Kurdish politician
- Ibrahim Akin, Turkish footballer
- Ibrahim Aydemir, Turkish footballer
- Ibrahim Ba, Senegalese-French footballer
- Ibrahim Bey, Egyptian Mamluk chieftain of Georgian origin
- Ibrahim Bilali, Kenyan boxer
- Ibrahim Ismail Chundrigar, Pakistani politician
- Ibrahim Fazeel, Maldivian footballer
- Ibrahim Ferrer, Afro-Cuban singer
- Ibrahim of Johor, Sultan of Johor, Malaysia
- Ibrahim Halidi, Prime Minister of Comoros
- Ibrahim Hashem, Jordanian lawyer and politician
- Ibrahim Heski, Kurdish politician
- Ibrahim Hussein, Kenya runner
- Ibrahim Kargbo, Sierra Leonean footballer
- Ibrahim Kas, Turkish footballer
- Ibrahim Maalouf, Lebanese jazz musician
- Ibrahim Meraachli, Lebanese actor
- Ibrahim Al-Mudhaf, Kuwaiti politician
- Ibrahim Haneef Muhammad, American voice actor
- Ibrahim Nagi, Egyptian poet
- Ibrahim Najjar, Lebanese politician
- Ibrahim Nasir, Maldivian politician
- Ibrahim Nasrallah, Palestinian poet
- Ibrahim Nooraddeen, Sultan of the Maldives
- Ibrahim Orabi, Egyptian wrestler
- Ibrahim Öztürk, Turkish footballer
- Ibrahim Pasha, several pashas named Ibrahim
- Ibrahim Rabimov, Tajikistani footballer
- Ibrahim Sahin, Turkish footballer
- Ibrahim Said, Egyptian footballer
- Ibrahim Al Shahrani, Saudi Arabian footballer
- Ibrahim Sidibe, Senegalese footballer

Chapter 1. THE MIDDLE EAST AND PALESTINE TO 1914: An Overview

India	India was an ecclesiastical province of the Church of the East, at least nominally, from the seventh to the sixteenth century. The Malabar Coast of India had long been home to a thriving East Syrian (Nestorian) Christian community, known as the St. Thomas Christians. The community traces its origins to the evangelical activity of Thomas the Apostle in the 1st century.
Germany	The Germany Pavilion is part of the World Showcase within Epcot at the Walt Disney World Resort.
	History
	The original design of the pavilion called for a boat ride along the Rhine river. It was to have focused on German folklore, in a similar manner to the Mexico and Norway rides.
Italy	The Italy Pavilion is a part of the World Showcase within Epcot at the Walt Disney World Resort.
	Layout
	The Italian Pavilion features a plaza surrounded by a collection of buildings evocative of Venetian, Florentine, and Roman architecture. Venetian architecture is represented by a re-creation of St Mark's Campanile (bell tower) and a replica of the Doge's Palace.
Allies	Allies is a Christian rock band. They released six albums during the 1980s and early 1990s.
	Band members
	The most notable band members were guitarist Randy Thomas, formerly of the Jesus music group Sweet Comfort Band and vocalist Bob Carlisle.

Chapter 2. OTTOMAN SOCIETY, PALESTINE, AND THE ORIGINS OF ZIONISM, 1800-1914

Aleppo	Aleppo is the largest city in Syria and the capital of Aleppo Governorate, the most populous Syrian governorate. With a population of 2,301,570 (2005 official estimate), it is also the largest city in the Levant.
	Aleppo is one of the oldest continuously inhabited cities in the world; it has been inhabited since perhaps as early as the 6th millennium BC. Excavations at Tell Qaramel (25 km north of Aleppo) show the area to have been inhabited since the 11th millennium BC, which makes it the oldest known human settlement in the world.
Baghdad	Baghdad is the capital of Iraq, as well as the coterminous Baghdad Governorate. With an estimated population between 7 and 7.5 million, it is the largest city in Iraq, the second largest city in the Arab World (after Cairo, Egypt), and the second largest city in Western Asia (after Tehran, Iran).
	Located along the Tigris River, the city was founded in the 8th century and became the capital of the Abbasid Caliphate.
Egypt	The Roman province of Egypt was established in 30 BC after Octavian (the future emperor Augustus) defeated his rival Mark Antony, deposed his lover Queen Cleopatra VII and annexed the Ptolemaic kingdom of Egypt to the Roman Empire. The province encompassed most of modern-day Egypt except for the Sinai Peninsula (which would later be conquered by Trajan). Aegyptus was bordered by the provinces of Creta et Cyrenaica to the West and Judaea to the East.
Greater Syria	Greater Syria, also known simply as Syria, is a term that denotes a region in the Near East bordering the Eastern Mediterranean Sea or the Levant.
	The classical Arabic name for Syria is Sham, which in later ages came to refer only to Damascus in Levantine Arabic, while the pre-Islamic name of the territory, Syria, was used again until the collapse of the Ottoman Empire in 1918.
	Historic Syria

The extent of the area known as Syria has changed over time.

Hebron

Hebron, is located in the southern West Bank, 30 km (19 mi) south of Jerusalem. Nestled in the Judean Mountains, it lies 930 meters (3,050 ft) above sea level. It is the largest city in the West Bank and home to around 165,000 Palestinians, and over 500 Jewish settlers concentrated in and around the old quarter.

| Ibrahim | Ibrahim is the Arabic name of the prophet Abraham. It is a common first name throughout the Muslim world. |

Given name

- Ibrahim I, Ottoman sultan
- Ibrahim Abatcha, Chadian politician
- Ibrahim Abouleish, Egyptian scientist
- Ibrahim Abu-Lughod, Palestinian academic
- Ibrahim Afellay, Dutch footballer
- Ibrahim Ahmad, Kurdish politician
- Ibrahim Akin, Turkish footballer
- Ibrahim Aydemir, Turkish footballer
- Ibrahim Ba, Senegalese-French footballer
- Ibrahim Bey, Egyptian Mamluk chieftain of Georgian origin
- Ibrahim Bilali, Kenyan boxer
- Ibrahim Ismail Chundrigar, Pakistani politician
- Ibrahim Fazeel, Maldivian footballer
- Ibrahim Ferrer, Afro-Cuban singer
- Ibrahim of Johor, Sultan of Johor, Malaysia
- Ibrahim Halidi, Prime Minister of Comoros
- Ibrahim Hashem, Jordanian lawyer and politician
- Ibrahim Heski, Kurdish politician
- Ibrahim Hussein, Kenya runner
- Ibrahim Kargbo, Sierra Leonean footballer
- Ibrahim Kas, Turkish footballer
- Ibrahim Maalouf, Lebanese jazz musician
- Ibrahim Meraachli, Lebanese actor
- Ibrahim Al-Mudhaf, Kuwaiti politician
- Ibrahim Haneef Muhammad, American voice actor
- Ibrahim Nagi, Egyptian poet
- Ibrahim Najjar, Lebanese politician
- Ibrahim Nasir, Maldivian politician
- Ibrahim Nasrallah, Palestinian poet
- Ibrahim Nooraddeen, Sultan of the Maldives
- Ibrahim Orabi, Egyptian wrestler
- Ibrahim Öztürk, Turkish footballer
- Ibrahim Pasha, several pashas named Ibrahim
- Ibrahim Rabimov, Tajikistani footballer
- Ibrahim Sahin, Turkish footballer
- Ibrahim Said, Egyptian footballer
- Ibrahim Al Shahrani, Saudi Arabian footballer
- Ibrahim Sidibe, Senegalese footballer

41

Chapter 2. OTTOMAN SOCIETY, PALESTINE, AND THE ORIGINS OF ZIONISM, 1800-1914

Muhammad	Muhammad ibn 'Abdullah (ca. 570/571 - June 8, 632), (Monday, 12th Rabi' al-Awwal, Year 11 A.H). is considered the founder of the religion of Islam, and is regarded by Muslims as a messenger and prophet of God, the last law-bearer in a series of Islamic prophets, and, by most Muslims, the last prophet of Islam as taught by the Qur'an. Muslims thus consider him the restorer of an uncorrupted original monotheistic faith (islam) of Adam, Noah, Abraham, Moses, Jesus and other prophets.
Ottoman Empire	The Ottoman Empire was an empire that lasted from 27 July 1299 to 29 October 1923.
	At the height of its power, in the 16th and 17th centuries, the empire spanned three continents, controlling much of Southeastern Europe, Western Asia and North Africa. The Ottoman Empire contained 29 provinces and numerous vassal states, some of which were later absorbed into the empire, while others were granted various types of autonomy during the course of centuries. The empire also temporarily gained authority over distant overseas lands through declarations of allegiance to the Ottoman Sultan and Caliph, such as the declaration by the Sultan of Aceh in 1565; or through the temporary acquisitions of islands in the Atlantic Ocean, such as Lanzarote in 1585.
Syria	Syria, officially the Syrian Arab Republic, is a country in Western Asia, bordering Lebanon and the Mediterranean Sea to the West, Turkey to the north, Iraq to the east, Jordan to the south, and Israel to the southwest.
	The name Syria formerly comprised the entire region of the Levant, while the modern state encompasses the site of several ancient kingdoms and empires, including the Eblan civilization of the third millennium BC. In the Islamic era, its capital city, Damascus, was the seat of the Umayyad Empire and a provincial capital of the Mamluk Empire. Damascus is one of the oldest continuously inhabited cities in the world.
Dhimmi	A dhimmi, (collectively ??? ????? ahl al-dhimmah, "the people of the dhimma or people of the contract") is a non-Muslim subject of a state governed in accordance with sharia law. The dhimma is a theoretical contract based on a widely held Islamic doctrine granting special status to adherents of Judaism, Christianity, and certain other non-Muslim religions ("People of the Book"). Dhimma provides rights of residence in return for taxes.

43

Chapter 2. OTTOMAN SOCIETY, PALESTINE, AND THE ORIGINS OF ZIONISM, 1800-1914

Histories	Histories is a book by Tacitus, written c. 100-110, which covers the Year of Four Emperors following the downfall of Nero, the rise of Vespasian, and the rule of the Flavian Dynasty (69-96) up to the death of Domitian.
	Subject matter
	In one of the first chapters of the Agricola Tacitus said that he wished to speak about the years of Domitian, of Nerva, and of Trajan. In the Historiae the project has been modified: in the introduction, Tacitus says that he will deal with the age of Nerva and Trajan at a later time.
Mandate	In Christian theology, a mandate is an order given from God that must be obeyed without question. For example, the mandate given to Abraham to offer his son Isaac as a sacrifice to God. (Genesis 22:1)
Palestine	Palestine (Greek: Παλαιστ?νη, Palaistine; Latin: Palaestina; Hebrew: ????????? Eretz-Yisra'el, (formerly also ????????, Palestina); Arabic: ??????? Filas?in, Falas?in, Filis?in) is a conventional name used, among others, to describe a geographic region between the Mediterranean Sea and the Jordan River, and various adjoining lands.
	Other terms for the same area include Canaan, Zion, the Land of Israel, and the Holy Land. Southern Levant is another purely geographic term, often implemented for the region, which does not have political or theologic implications.
Al-Islah	Al-Islah, is a political party in Yemen that is absent from the Yemeni parliament. According to Al Jazeera, its ideology is partly based on Islamism. One of its main leaders is Tawakel Karman, who is also a member of parliament for the similarly named Al-Islah party that has 46 parliamentary seats.

Chapter 2. OTTOMAN SOCIETY, PALESTINE, AND THE ORIGINS OF ZIONISM, 1800-1914

Zionism	Zionism is a Jewish political movement that, in its broadest sense, has supported the self-determination of the Jewish people in a sovereign Jewish national homeland. Since the establishment of the State of Israel, the Zionist movement continues primarily to advocate on behalf of the Jewish state and address threats to its continued existence and security. In a less common usage, the term may also refer to 1) non-political, Cultural Zionism, founded and represented most prominently by Ahad Ha'am; and 2) political support for the State of Israel by non-Jews, as in Christian Zionism.
Damascus	Damascus is the capital and the second largest city of Syria as well as one of the country's 14 governorates. The Damascus Governorate is ruled by a governor appointed by the Minister of Interior. In addition to being the oldest continuously inhabited city in the world, Damascus is a major cultural and religious center of the Levant.
Paris	Paris, the son of Priam, king of Troy, appears in a number of Greek legends. Probably the best-known was his elopement with Helen, queen of Sparta, this being one of the immediate causes of the Trojan War. Later in the war, he fatally wounds Achilles in the heel with an arrow, as foretold by Achilles's mother, Thetis.
Politics	Aristotle's Politics is a work of political philosophy. The end of the Nicomachean Ethics declared that the inquiry into ethics necessarily follows into politics, and the two works are frequently considered to be parts of a larger treatise, or perhaps connected lectures, dealing with the "philosophy of human affairs." The title of the Politics literally means "the things concerning the polis."
	Composition
	The literary character of the Politics is subject to some dispute, growing out of the textual difficulties that attended the loss of Aristotle's works. Book III ends with a sentence that is repeated almost verbatim at the start of Book VII, while the intervening Books IV-VI seem to have a very different flavor from the rest; Book IV seems to refer several times back to the discussion of the best regime contained in Books VII-VIII. Some editors have therefore inserted Books VII-VIII after Book III. At the same time, however, references to the "discourses on politics" that occur in the Nicomachean Ethics suggest that the treatise as a whole ought to conclude with the discussion of education that occurs in Book VIII of the Politics, although it is not certain that Aristotle is referring to the Politics here.

Chapter 2. OTTOMAN SOCIETY, PALESTINE, AND THE ORIGINS OF ZIONISM, 1800-1914

Response	A response is the second half of one of a set of preces, the said or sung answer by the congregation or choir to a versicle said or sung by an officiant or cantor. In the following opening of the Anglican service of Evening Prayer according to the Book of Common Prayer (BCP), the first line is the versicle and the second is the response.
	In some liturgical books (such as hymnals or breviaries) the symbol "R/" or "?" is used to denote a response.
Al-Islah	Al-Islah, is a political party in Yemen that is absent from the Yemeni parliament. According to Al Jazeera, its ideology is partly based on Islamism. One of its main leaders is Tawakel Karman, who is also a member of parliament for the similarly named Al-Islah party that has 46 parliamentary seats.
Iraq	Iraq ; officially the Republic of Iraq is a country in Western Asia spanning most of the northwestern end of the Zagros mountain range, the eastern part of the Syrian Desert and the northern part of the Arabian Desert.
	Iraq is bordered by Jordan to the west, Syria to the northwest, Turkey to the north, Iran to the east, and Kuwait and Saudi Arabia to the south. Iraq has a narrow section of coastline measuring 58 km (35 miles) on the northern Persian Gulf.
Mesopotamia	Mesopotamia was the name of two distinct Roman provinces, the one a short-lived creation of the Roman Emperor Trajan in 116-117 and the other established by Emperor Septimius Severus in ca. 198, which lasted until the Muslim conquests of the 7th century.
	Trajan's province
	In 113, Emperor Trajan (r. 98-117) launched a war against Rome's long-time eastern rival, the Parthian Empire. In 114, he conquered Armenia, which was made into a province, and by the end of 115, he had conquered northern Mesopotamia.

Chapter 2. OTTOMAN SOCIETY, PALESTINE, AND THE ORIGINS OF ZIONISM, 1800-1914

Ancients	The Ancients were a group of English artists who were brought together by their attraction to archaism in art and admiration for the work of William Blake. The core members of the Ancients were Samuel Palmer, George Richmond, Edward Calvert. They met in Blake's apartment, dubbed the "House of Interpreter" and at the home of Samuel Palmer in the Kent village of Shoreham.
Arab Revolt	The Arab Revolt was initiated by the Sherif Hussein bin Ali with the aim of securing independence from the ruling Ottoman Turks and creating a single unified Arab state spanning from Aleppo in Syria to Aden in Yemen.

The rise of nationalism under the Ottoman Empire goes back to 1821. Arab nationalism has its roots in the Mashriq, particularly in countries of Sham (the Levant). The political orientation of Arab nationalists in the years prior to the Great War was generally moderate. |
| Galilee | Galilee, is a large region in northern Israel which overlaps with much of the administrative North District of the country. Traditionally divided into Upper Galilee, Lower Galilee, and Western Galilee, extending from Dan to the north, at the base of Mount Hermon, along Mount Lebanon to the ridges of Mount Carmel and Mount Gilboa to the south, and from the Jordan Rift Valley to the east across the plains of the Jezreel Valley and Acre to the shores of the Mediterranean Sea and the Coastal Plain in the west.

Most of Galilee consists of rocky terrain, at heights of between 500 and 700 metres. |
| Jaffa | Jaffa is an ancient port city believed to be one of the oldest in the world. Jaffa has been incorporated with Tel Aviv creating the city of Tel Aviv-Yafo, Israel.

Etymology

The name of the city is supposedly mentioned in Egyptian sources and the Amarna Letters as Yapu. |

51

Chapter 2. OTTOMAN SOCIETY, PALESTINE, AND THE ORIGINS OF ZIONISM, 1800-1914

Christian	A Christian is a person who adheres to Christianity, an Abrahamic, monotheistic religion based on the life and teachings of Jesus of Nazareth as recorded in the Canonical gospels and the letters of the New Testament. Central to the Christian faith is love or Agape. Christians also believe Jesus is the Messiah prophesied in the Hebrew Bible, the Son of God, and the savior of mankind from their sins.
Pilgrim	Pilgrims (US), or Pilgrim Fathers (UK), is a name commonly applied to early settlers of the Plymouth Colony in present-day Plymouth, Massachusetts, United States. Their leadership came from the religious congregations of English Dissenters who had fled the volatile political environment in the East Midlands of England for the relative calm and tolerance of Holland in the Netherlands. Concerned with losing their cultural identity, the group later arranged with English investors to establish a new colony in North America. The colony, established in 1620, became the oldest continuously inhabited British settlement and the second successful English settlement (after the founding of Jamestown, Virginia in 1607) in what was to become the United States of America. The Pilgrims' story of seeking religious freedom has become a central theme of the history and culture of the United States.
Christianity	Christianity is a monotheistic religion based on the life and teachings of Jesus as presented in canonical gospels and other New Testament writings. Adherents of the Christian faith are known as Christians. Mainstream Christianity teaches that the Greatest commandment is love or Agape.
Hama	Hama is a city on the banks of the Orontes River in central Syria north of Damascus. It is the provincial capital of the Hama Governorate. The city is the location of the historical city Hamath.
Judea	35°18′23″E? / ?31.69889°N 35.30639°E

53

Judea, when Roman Judea was renamed Syria Palaestina following the Jewish Bar Kokhba revolt.

Etymology

The name Judea is a Greek and Roman adaptation of the name "Judah", which originally encompassed the territory of the Israelite tribe of that name and later of the ancient Kingdom of Judah. It was the name in use in English throughout history until the Jordanian occupation of the area.

Samaria	Samaria is a term used for a mountainous region roughly corresponding to the northern part of the West Bank. According to 1 Kings 16:24, it is derived from the individual [or clan] Shemer, from whom Omri purchased the site. The name was the only name used for this area from ancient times until the Jordanian conquest of 1948, at which point the Jordanian occupiers coined the term West Bank.
West Bank	The West Bank of the Jordan River is the landlocked geographical eastern part of the Palestinian territories located in the Western Asia. To the west, north, and south, the West Bank shares borders with the state of Israel. To the east, across the Jordan River, lies the Hashemite Kingdom of Jordan.
Western	Western is a Franco-Belgian one shot comic written by Jean Van Hamme, illustrated by Grzegorz Rosinski and published by Le Lombard in French and Cinebook in English.

Story

Volume

- Western - May 2001 ISBN 2-80361-662-9

Translations

Cinebook Ltd plans to publish Western in June 2011

Chapter 2. OTTOMAN SOCIETY, PALESTINE, AND THE ORIGINS OF ZIONISM, 1800-1914

Bilu	Bilu was a movement whose goal was the agricultural settlement of the Land of Israel. "Bilu" is an acronym based on a verse from the Book of Isaiah (2:5) "??? ???? ??? ?????" Beit Ya'akov Lekhu Venelkha ("House of Jacob, let us go [up]"). It's members were known as the Bilu'im.
Temple	In the Latter Day Saint movement, a temple is a building dedicated to be a house of God and is reserved for special forms of worship. A temple differs from a church meetinghouse, which is used for weekly worship services. Temples have been a significant part of the Latter Day Saint movement since early in its inception.
Temple Mount	The Temple Mount, also known in the Bible as Mount Moriah (some also identify it with the biblical Mount Zion) and by Muslims as the Noble Sanctuary (Bait-ul-Muqaddas), is a religious site in the Old City of Jerusalem. Judaism regards the Temple Mount as the place where God chose the Divine Presence to rest (Isa 8:18); it was from here the world expanded into its present form and where God gathered the dust used to create the first man, Adam.{According to the sages of the Talmud[13]} The site is the location of Abraham's binding of Isaac, and of two Jewish Temples. According to the Bible the site should function as the center of all national life - government, judicial and, of course, religious center (Deut 12:5-26; 14:23-25; 15:20; 16:2-16; 17:8-10; 26: 2; 31: 11; Isa 2: 2-5; Oba 1:21; Psa 48) .
Hovevei Zion	Hovevei Zion, refers to organizations that are now considered the forerunners and foundation-builders of modern Zionism. Many of these first groups were established in Eastern European countries in the early 1880s with the aim to promote Jewish immigration to the Land of Israel, then a part of Ottoman Empire, and advance Jewish settlement there, particularly agricultural. Most of them stayed away from politics.

Chapter 2. OTTOMAN SOCIETY, PALESTINE, AND THE ORIGINS OF ZIONISM, 1800-1914

East Jerusalem	East Jerusalem refers to the parts of Jerusalem captured by Jordan in the 1948 Arab-Israeli War and then taken by Israel in the 1967 Six-Day War. It includes Jerusalem's Old City and some of the holiest sites of Judaism, Christianity, and Islam, such as the Temple Mount, Western Wall, Al-Aqsa Mosque, and the Church of the Holy Sepulchre. The term "East Jerusalem" may refer to either the area under Jordanian rule between 1949 and 1967 which was incorporated into the municipality of Jerusalem after 1967, covering some 70 km^2 (27 sq mi), or the territory of the pre-1967 Jordanian municipality, covering 6.4 km^2 (2.5 sq mi).
Jerusalem	Jerusalem [ii] is the capital of Israel, though not internationally recognized as such.[iii] If the area and population of East Jerusalem is included, it is Israel's largest city in both population and area, with a population of 763,800 residents over an area of 125.1 km^2 (48.3 sq mi).[iv] Located in the Judean Mountains, between the Mediterranean Sea and the northern edge of the Dead Sea, modern Jerusalem has grown far beyond the boundaries of the Old City.
	Jerusalem is a holy city to the three major Abrahamic religions--Judaism, Christianity and Islam. In Judaism, Jerusalem has been the holiest city since, according to the Torah, King David of Israel first established it as the capital of the united Kingdom of Israel in c. 1000 BCE, and his son Solomon commissioned the building of the First Temple in the city.
Impact	Impact is a monthly magazine published in the United Kingdom. It covers the field of action entertainment: including Hong Kong action cinema, worldwide martial arts films, Hollywood productions, anime, comics, action films and East Asian cinema in general. Originally founded and edited by Bey Logan, it is presently edited by John Mosby, with Mike Leeder acting as Eastern Editor from the Hong Kong office, and Andrez Bergen as Tokyo Correspondent.
World	WORLD Magazine is a biweekly Christian news magazine, published in the United States of America by God's World Publications, a non-profit 501(c)(3) organization based in Asheville, North Carolina. WORLD differs from most other news magazines in that its declared perspective is one of conservative evangelical Protestantism. Its mission statement is "To report, interpret, and illustrate the news in a timely, accurate, enjoyable, and arresting fashion from a perspective committed to the Bible as the inerrant Word of God."
	Each issue features both U.S. and international news, cultural analysis, editorials and commentary, as well as book, music and movie reviews.

Chapter 2. OTTOMAN SOCIETY, PALESTINE, AND THE ORIGINS OF ZIONISM, 1800-1914

Barak	Barak, Al-Buraq the son of Abinoam from Kedesh in Naphtali, was a military general in the Book of Judges in the Bible. He was the commander of the army of Deborah, the prophetess and heroine of the Hebrew Bible. Barak and Deborah are credited with defeating the Canaanite armies led by Sisera, who for twenty years had oppressed the Israelites.
Ehud	Ehud ben-Gera is described in the Biblical Book of Judges as a judge who was sent by God to deliver the Israelites from the Moabite yoke.
	Ehud was sent to the Moabite King Eglon on the pretext of delivering the Israelites' annual tribute. He had blacksmiths make a double-edged shortsword about eighteen inches long, useful for a stabbing thrust.
Labor Zionism	Labor Zionism can be described as the major stream of the left wing of the Zionist movement. It was, for many years, the most significant tendency among Zionists and Zionist organizational structure. It saw itself as the Zionist sector of the historic Jewish labor movements of Eastern and Central Europe, eventually developing local units in most countries with sizeable Jewish populations.
Lebanon	Lebanon is a mural size painting by Nabil Kanso depicting the Lebanese Civil War in a scene invoking the spirit and character of the people in the midst of horror and violence gripping the country. Amid the scene of chaos and devastation, two central figures reach across toward each other symbolically to represent the appeal for unity in defiance of the forces of division, destruction, and terror.
	Description
	Painted in oil on linen and completed in 1983, the painting Lebanon measures 28 feet (8.5 meters) long by 10 feet (3meters) tall.

Chapter 2. OTTOMAN SOCIETY, PALESTINE, AND THE ORIGINS OF ZIONISM, 1800-1914

Sultan	Sultan is a title, with several historical meanings. Originally, it was an Arabic language abstract noun meaning "strength", "authority", or "rulership", derived from the masdar ???? sul?ah, meaning "authority" or "power". Later, it came to be used as the title of certain rulers who claimed almost full sovereignty in practical terms (i.e. the lack of dependence on any higher ruler), without claiming the overall caliphate, or it was used to refer to a powerful governor of a province within the caliphate.
Filastin	Filastin was a twice-weekly newspaper published from 1911-1948 in Palestine. Published from Jaffa, the principal publishers (who edited and owned the paper) were Isa al-Isa and his cousin Yusef al-Isa. Both al-Isas were Greek Orthodox, opponents of British administration, and supporters of pan-Arab unity.
Al-Karmil	Al-Karmil was a weekly Arabic language newspaper founded toward the end of Ottoman imperial rule in Palestine. Named for Mount Carmel in the Haifa district, the first issue was published in December 1908, with the stated purpose of "opposing Zionist colonization". The owner, editor and key writer for the newspaper was Najib Nassar, a Palestinian Christian and staunch anti-Zionist, whose editorials warning of the dangers posed by Zionism to the Palestinian people were often reprinted in other Syrian newspapers.

Chapter 3. WORLD WAR I, GREAT BRITAIN, AND THE PEACE SETTLEMENTS, 1914-1921

Abbasid Caliphate	The Abbasid caliphate, more simply, the Abbasids, was the third of the Islamic caliphates. It was ruled by the Abbasid dynasty of caliphs, who built their capital in Baghdad after overthrowing the Umayyad caliphs from all but the Al Andalus region. The Abbasid caliphate was founded by the descendants of the Islamic prophet Muhammad's youngest uncle, Abbas ibn Abd al-Muttalib, in Harran in 750 CE and shifted its capital in 762 to Baghdad.
Baghdad	Baghdad is the capital of Iraq, as well as the coterminous Baghdad Governorate. With an estimated population between 7 and 7.5 million, it is the largest city in Iraq, the second largest city in the Arab World (after Cairo, Egypt), and the second largest city in Western Asia (after Tehran, Iran). Located along the Tigris River, the city was founded in the 8th century and became the capital of the Abbasid Caliphate.
Caliphate	The term caliphate "dominion of a caliph ('successor,')," refers to the first system of government established in Islam, and represented the political unity of the Muslim Ummah (nation). In theory, it is a constitutional republic , meaning that the head of state (the Caliph) and other officials are dicate to the people according to Islamic law, which exercises power over their citizens. It was initially led by Muhammad's disciples as a continuation of the political system the prophet established, known as the 'rashidun caliphates'.
Catholic	The word catholic comes from the Greek phrase καθ?λου (kath'holou), meaning "on the whole," "according to the whole" or "in general", and is a combination of the Greek words κατ? meaning "about" and ?λος meaning "whole". The word in English can mean either "including a wide variety of things; all-embracing" or "of the Roman Catholic faith." as "relating to the historic doctrine and practice of the Western Church."

	It was first used to describe the Christian Church in the early 2nd century to emphasize its universal scope. In the context of Christian ecclesiology, it has a rich history and several usages.
Germany	The Germany Pavilion is part of the World Showcase within Epcot at the Walt Disney World Resort.
	History
	The original design of the pavilion called for a boat ride along the Rhine river. It was to have focused on German folklore, in a similar manner to the Mexico and Norway rides.
Hama	Hama is a city on the banks of the Orontes River in central Syria north of Damascus. It is the provincial capital of the Hama Governorate. The city is the location of the historical city Hamath.
Iraq	Iraq ; officially the Republic of Iraq is a country in Western Asia spanning most of the northwestern end of the Zagros mountain range, the eastern part of the Syrian Desert and the northern part of the Arabian Desert.
	Iraq is bordered by Jordan to the west, Syria to the northwest, Turkey to the north, Iran to the east, and Kuwait and Saudi Arabia to the south. Iraq has a narrow section of coastline measuring 58 km (35 miles) on the northern Persian Gulf.
Lebanon	Lebanon is a mural size painting by Nabil Kanso depicting the Lebanese Civil War in a scene invoking the spirit and character of the people in the midst of horror and violence gripping the country. Amid the scene of chaos and devastation, two central figures reach across toward each other symbolically to represent the appeal for unity in defiance of the forces of division, destruction, and terror.
	Description

67

	Painted in oil on linen and completed in 1983, the painting Lebanon measures 28 feet (8.5 meters) long by 10 feet (3meters) tall.
Mosul	43°07'0"E? / ?36.366667°N 43.116667°E
	Mosul (Arabic: ??????? al-Maw?il, Ma?lawi Arabic: al-Mo?ul, Syriac: ????? (Nînwe), Kurdish: Mûsil/Nînewe is a city in northern Iraq and the capital of the Ninawa Governorate, some 400 km (250 miles) northwest of Baghdad. The original city stands on the west bank of the Tigris River, opposite the ancient Assyrian city of Nineveh on the east bank, but the metropolitan area has now grown to encompass substantial areas on both banks, with five bridges linking the two sides. The majority of its population is now Arab (with Kurdish, Assyrians, Turcoman and Armenian minorities).
Ottoman Empire	The Ottoman Empire was an empire that lasted from 27 July 1299 to 29 October 1923.
	At the height of its power, in the 16th and 17th centuries, the empire spanned three continents, controlling much of Southeastern Europe, Western Asia and North Africa. The Ottoman Empire contained 29 provinces and numerous vassal states, some of which were later absorbed into the empire, while others were granted various types of autonomy during the course of centuries. The empire also temporarily gained authority over distant overseas lands through declarations of allegiance to the Ottoman Sultan and Caliph, such as the declaration by the Sultan of Aceh in 1565; or through the temporary acquisitions of islands in the Atlantic Ocean, such as Lanzarote in 1585.
Syria	Syria, officially the Syrian Arab Republic, is a country in Western Asia, bordering Lebanon and the Mediterranean Sea to the West, Turkey to the north, Iraq to the east, Jordan to the south, and Israel to the southwest.

The name Syria formerly comprised the entire region of the Levant, while the modern state encompasses the site of several ancient kingdoms and empires, including the Eblan civilization of the third millennium BC. In the Islamic era, its capital city, Damascus, was the seat of the Umayyad Empire and a provincial capital of the Mamluk Empire. Damascus is one of the oldest continuously inhabited cities in the world.

World

WORLD Magazine is a biweekly Christian news magazine, published in the United States of America by God's World Publications, a non-profit 501(c)(3) organization based in Asheville, North Carolina. WORLD differs from most other news magazines in that its declared perspective is one of conservative evangelical Protestantism. Its mission statement is "To report, interpret, and illustrate the news in a timely, accurate, enjoyable, and arresting fashion from a perspective committed to the Bible as the inerrant Word of God."

Each issue features both U.S. and international news, cultural analysis, editorials and commentary, as well as book, music and movie reviews.

Alliance

This article incorporates text from Easton's Bible Dictionary (1897), a publication now in the public domain.

Abraham formed an alliance with some of the Canaanitish princes (Gen. 14:13), also with Abimelech (21:22-32). Joshua and the elders of Israel entered into an alliance with the Gibeonites (Josh. 9:3-27). When the Israelites entered Canaan they were forbidden to enter into alliances with the inhabitants of the country (Lev. 18:3, 4; 20:22, 23).

Allies

Allies is a Christian rock band. They released six albums during the 1980s and early 1990s.

Band members

The most notable band members were guitarist Randy Thomas, formerly of the Jesus music group Sweet Comfort Band and vocalist Bob Carlisle.

Politics	Aristotle's Politics is a work of political philosophy. The end of the Nicomachean Ethics declared that the inquiry into ethics necessarily follows into politics, and the two works are frequently considered to be parts of a larger treatise, or perhaps connected lectures, dealing with the "philosophy of human affairs." The title of the Politics literally means "the things concerning the polis." Composition The literary character of the Politics is subject to some dispute, growing out of the textual difficulties that attended the loss of Aristotle's works. Book III ends with a sentence that is repeated almost verbatim at the start of Book VII, while the intervening Books IV-VI seem to have a very different flavor from the rest; Book IV seems to refer several times back to the discussion of the best regime contained in Books VII-VIII. Some editors have therefore inserted Books VII-VIII after Book III. At the same time, however, references to the "discourses on politics" that occur in the Nicomachean Ethics suggest that the treatise as a whole ought to conclude with the discussion of education that occurs in Book VIII of the Politics, although it is not certain that Aristotle is referring to the Politics here.
India	India was an ecclesiastical province of the Church of the East, at least nominally, from the seventh to the sixteenth century. The Malabar Coast of India had long been home to a thriving East Syrian (Nestorian) Christian community, known as the St. Thomas Christians. The community traces its origins to the evangelical activity of Thomas the Apostle in the 1st century.
Palestine	Palestine (Greek: Παλαιστ?νη, Palaistine; Latin: Palaestina; Hebrew: ????????? Eretz-Yisra'el, (formerly also ????????, Palestina); Arabic: ??????? Filas?in, Falas?in, Filis?in) is a conventional name used, among others, to describe a geographic region between the Mediterranean Sea and the Jordan River, and various adjoining lands. Other terms for the same area include Canaan, Zion, the Land of Israel, and the Holy Land. Southern Levant is another purely geographic term, often implemented for the region, which does not have political or theologic implications.

73

Chapter 3. WORLD WAR I, GREAT BRITAIN, AND THE PEACE SETTLEMENTS, 1914-1921

Henry	Henry is an English male given name and a surname, from the Old French Henry derived itself from the Germanic name Haimric, which was derived from the word elements haim, meaning "home" and ric, meaning "power, ruler". Harry, its English short form, was considered the "spoken form" of Henry in medieval England. Most English kings named Henry were called Harry.
Samuel	Samuel is a leader of ancient Israel in the Books of Samuel in the Hebrew Bible. He is also known as a prophet and is mentioned in the Qur'an. His status, as viewed by rabbinical literature, is that he was the last of the Hebrew Judges and the first of the major prophets who began to prophesy inside the Land of Israel.
Abdullah	Abdullah is a common Arabic male name. Humility before Allah is an essential value of Islam, hence Abdullah is a favorite name among Muslims. It was once common among Arabic-speaking Jews as well, especially Iraqi Jews.
Husayn	Husayn is an Arabic name which is the diminutive of Hassan, meaning "good", "handsome" or "beautiful". It is commonly given as a male given name among Muslims, in honor of Husayn ibn Ali (626-680 AD). In some Persian sources the forms ?osayn, Hosayn, or Hossein is used.
Italy	The Italy Pavilion is a part of the World Showcase within Epcot at the Walt Disney World Resort. Layout The Italian Pavilion features a plaza surrounded by a collection of buildings evocative of Venetian, Florentine, and Roman architecture. Venetian architecture is represented by a re-creation of St Mark's Campanile (bell tower) and a replica of the Doge's Palace.
Sharif	Sharif or Chérif is a traditional Arab tribal title given to those who serve as the protector of the tribe and all tribal assets, such as property, wells, and land. In origin, the word is an adjective meaning "noble", "highborn". The feminine singular is sharifa(h) (.

Chapter 3. WORLD WAR I, GREAT BRITAIN, AND THE PEACE SETTLEMENTS, 1914-1921

Transjordan	The Transjordan is a section of the land of Israel mentioned in the Hebrew Bible. It is the land east of the Jordan River in which the tribes of Reuben and Gad, and half the tribe of Manasseh settle. Name The prefix trans- is Latin and means "across" or beyond, and so "Transjordan" refers to the land on the other side of the Jordan River.
Correspondence	In theology, correspondence is the relationship between spiritual and natural realities, or between mental and physical realities. The term was coined by the 18th century theologian Emanuel Swedenborg in his Arcana Coelestia (1749-1756) and Heaven and Hell (1758) and other works. Swedenborg states that there is a correspondence between, for example: thought and speech, between intention and action, between mind and body, and between God and creation.
Arab Revolt	The Arab Revolt was initiated by the Sherif Hussein bin Ali with the aim of securing independence from the ruling Ottoman Turks and creating a single unified Arab state spanning from Aleppo in Syria to Aden in Yemen. The rise of nationalism under the Ottoman Empire goes back to 1821. Arab nationalism has its roots in the Mashriq, particularly in countries of Sham (the Levant). The political orientation of Arab nationalists in the years prior to the Great War was generally moderate.
Mandate	In Christian theology, a mandate is an order given from God that must be obeyed without question. For example, the mandate given to Abraham to offer his son Isaac as a sacrifice to God. (Genesis 22:1)

Chapter 3. WORLD WAR I, GREAT BRITAIN, AND THE PEACE SETTLEMENTS, 1914-1921

Arabia	Arabia was a satrapy (province) of the Achaemenid Empire and later of the Sassanid Empire, by the name of Arabistan. Achaemenid Era Achaemenid Arabia corresponded to the lands between Egypt and Mesopotamia, known as Arabia Petraea. According to Herodotus, the Cambyses did not subdue the Arabs when he attacked Egypt in 525 BCE. His successor Darius the Great does not mention the Arabs in the Behistun inscription from the first years of his reign, but mentions them in later texts.
Emir	Emir, ("commander" or "general", also "prince" ; also transliterated as amir, aamir or ameer) is a high title of nobility or office, used throughout the Muslim world. Emirs are usually considered high-ranking sheikhs, but in monarchical states the term is also used for princes, with "Emirate" being analogous to principality in this sense. While emir is the predominant spelling in English and many other languages, amir, closer to the original Arabic, is more common for its numerous compounds (e.g. admiral) and in individual names.
Saudi Arabia	The Kingdom of Saudi Arabia, commonly known as Saudi Arabia is, in land area, the third largest Arab country and the largest country in the Middle East. It is bordered by Jordan and Iraq on the north and northeast, Kuwait, Qatar and the United Arab Emirates on the east, Oman on the southeast, and Yemen on the south. It is also connected to Bahrain by the King Fahd Causeway.
Aleppo	Aleppo is the largest city in Syria and the capital of Aleppo Governorate, the most populous Syrian governorate. With a population of 2,301,570 (2005 official estimate), it is also the largest city in the Levant.

	Aleppo is one of the oldest continuously inhabited cities in the world; it has been inhabited since perhaps as early as the 6th millennium BC. Excavations at Tell Qaramel (25 km north of Aleppo) show the area to have been inhabited since the 11th millennium BC, which makes it the oldest known human settlement in the world.
Zionism	Zionism is a Jewish political movement that, in its broadest sense, has supported the self-determination of the Jewish people in a sovereign Jewish national homeland. Since the establishment of the State of Israel, the Zionist movement continues primarily to advocate on behalf of the Jewish state and address threats to its continued existence and security. In a less common usage, the term may also refer to 1) non-political, Cultural Zionism, founded and represented most prominently by Ahad Ha'am; and 2) political support for the State of Israel by non-Jews, as in Christian Zionism.
Arab	The proper name Arab or "Arabian" (and cognates in other languages) has been used to translate several different but similar sounding words in ancient and classical texts which do not necessarily have the same meaning or origin. Grunebaum, in his book Classical Islam said that an approximate translation is "passerby" or "nomad". Will Durant, in The Age of Faith, said that Arab meant Arid.
Ariel	Ariel is an Israeli settlement and a city in the central West Bank. Established in 1978, its population at the end of 2009 was 17,600, including 7,000 immigrants who came to Israel after 1990. It is the fourth largest Jewish settlement city in the West Bank., after Modi'in Illit, Beitar Illit, and Ma'ale Adumim.

In Hebrew, Ariel, literally means 'Lion of God'. |
| State | The term state is used in various senses by Catholic theologians and spiritual writers.

It may be taken to signify a profession or calling in life, as where St. Paul says, in I Corinthians 7:20: "Let every man abide in the same calling in which he was called". States are classified in the Catholic Church as the clerical state, the religious state, and the secular state; and among religious states, again, we have those of the contemplative, the active, and the mixed orders. |

Response	A response is the second half of one of a set of preces, the said or sung answer by the congregation or choir to a versicle said or sung by an officiant or cantor. In the following opening of the Anglican service of Evening Prayer according to the Book of Common Prayer (BCP), the first line is the versicle and the second is the response. In some liturgical books (such as hymnals or breviaries) the symbol "R/" or "?" is used to denote a response.
Tripartite	In Christian theology, the tripartite viewpoint holds that man is a composite of three distinct components: body, soul and spirit. It is less popular than the bipartite view, where "soul" and "spirit" are taken as different terms for the same entity. Scriptural Basis The two primary proof texts for this position are as follows: 1 Thessalonians 5:23 Proponents of the tripartite view claim that this verse spells out clearly the three components of the human, emphasized by the descriptors of "whole" and "completely." Opponents argue that spirit and soul are merely a repetition of synonyms, a common form used elsewhere in scripture to add the idea completeness.
Walter	Walter is a masculine given name, from an Old High German Walthari, containing the elements wald "rule" and hari "army, warrior". The latizined form is Waltharius, the title of a poem on the legendary Gothic king Walter of Aquitaine. A fragmentary Old English poem on the same character is known as Waldere.

Chapter 3. WORLD WAR I, GREAT BRITAIN, AND THE PEACE SETTLEMENTS, 1914-1921

Arafat	Arafat is a surname or given name, and may refer to: • Yasser Arafat • Fathi Arafat Palestinian physician • Moussa Arafat cousin of Yasser Arafat • Raed Arafat Romanian physician • Suha Arafat widow of Yasser Arafat • Yasir Arafat , Pakistani cricketer .
British Arabs	British Arabs are people in the United Kingdom who were born in or have ancestry from the Arab World. Unlike Black British or Asian British, the term is not one of those employed in government ethnicity categorisations used in the census and for national statistics. It is, however, the term used by the National Association of British Arabs and has also been employed by academics and in the media.
Anglo-French Declaration	The Anglo-French Declaration was signed between France and Great Britain on November 7, 1918 agreeing to implement a "complete and final liberation" of countries that had been part of the Ottoman Empire including the establishment of democratic governments in Syria and Mesopotamia. The agreement made it explicit that the form of the new governments was to be determined by local populations rather than imposed by the signatory powers. The agreement was meant to allay Arab suspicions of possible European colonialist or imperialist ambitions.
Declaration to the Seven	The Declaration to the Seven was a document written by Sir Henry McMahon and released by the British Government in response to a memorandum issued anonymously by seven Syrian notables in Cairo who were members of the newly-formed Party of Syrian Unity, which had been established in the wake of the Balfour Declaration of 1917 and the publication by the Bolsheviks of the secret Sykes-Picot Agreement. The memorandum requested a "guarantee of the ultimate independence of Arabia". The Declaration stated the British policy that the future government of the regions of the Ottoman Empire occupied by Allied forces in World War I should be based on the consent of the governed.
Peace	Peace is an Athenian Old Comedy written and produced by the Greek playwright Aristophanes. It won second prize at the City Dionysia where it was staged just a few days before the ratification of the Peace of Nicias (421 BC), which promised to end the ten year old Peloponnesian War. The play is notable for its joyous anticipation of peace and for its celebration of a return to an idyllic life in the countryside.

Chapter 3. WORLD WAR I, GREAT BRITAIN, AND THE PEACE SETTLEMENTS, 1914-1921

Mandate	In Christian theology, a mandate is an order given from God that must be obeyed without question. For example, the mandate given to Abraham to offer his son Isaac as a sacrifice to God. (Genesis 22:1)
Arab world	The Arab world refers to Arabic-speaking countries stretching from the Atlantic Ocean in the west to the Arabian Sea in the east, and from the Mediterranean Sea in the north to the Horn of Africa and the Indian Ocean in the southeast. It consists of 22 countries and territories with a combined population of 360 million people straddling North Africa and Western Asia. The sentiment of Arab nationalism arose in the second half of the 19th century along with other nationalisms within the failing Ottoman Empire.
Egypt	The Roman province of Egypt was established in 30 BC after Octavian (the future emperor Augustus) defeated his rival Mark Antony, deposed his lover Queen Cleopatra VII and annexed the Ptolemaic kingdom of Egypt to the Roman Empire. The province encompassed most of modern-day Egypt except for the Sinai Peninsula (which would later be conquered by Trajan). Aegyptus was bordered by the provinces of Creta et Cyrenaica to the West and Judaea to the East.
Aqaba	Aqaba is a coastal town in the far south of Jordan. It is the capital of Aqaba Governorate. Aqaba is strategically important to Jordan as it is the country's only seaport.
The Palestine Mandate	The Palestine Mandate, was a legal commission for the administration of Palestine, the draft of which was formally confirmed by the Council of the League of Nations on 24 July 1922 and which came into effect on 26 September 1923 The mandate formalised British rule in the Southern part of Ottoman Syria from 1923-1948. With the League of Nations' consent on 16 September 1922, the UK divided the Mandate territory into two administrative areas, Palestine, under direct British rule, and autonomous Transjordan, under the rule of the Hashemite family from Hijaz Saudi Arabia, in accordance with the McMahon Pledge of 1915. Transjordan was exempt from the Mandate provisions concerning the Jewish National Home. The preamble of the mandate declared:

Chapter 3. WORLD WAR I, GREAT BRITAIN, AND THE PEACE SETTLEMENTS, 1914-1921

Whereas the Principal Allied Powers have also agreed that the Mandatory should be responsible for putting into effect the declaration originally made on November 2nd, 1917, by the Government of His Britannic Majesty, and adopted by the said Powers, in favour of the establishment in Palestine of a national home for the Jewish people, it being clearly understood that nothing should be done which might prejudice the civil and religious rights of existing non-Jewish communities in Palestine, or the rights and political status enjoyed by Jews in any other country.

Chapter 4. PALESTINE BETWEEN THE WARS

Jerusalem	Jerusalem [ii] is the capital of Israel, though not internationally recognized as such.[iii] If the area and population of East Jerusalem is included, it is Israel's largest city in both population and area, with a population of 763,800 residents over an area of 125.1 km^2 (48.3 sq mi).[iv] Located in the Judean Mountains, between the Mediterranean Sea and the northern edge of the Dead Sea, modern Jerusalem has grown far beyond the boundaries of the Old City. Jerusalem is a holy city to the three major Abrahamic religions--Judaism, Christianity and Islam. In Judaism, Jerusalem has been the holiest city since, according to the Torah, King David of Israel first established it as the capital of the united Kingdom of Israel in c. 1000 BCE, and his son Solomon commissioned the building of the First Temple in the city.
Mandate	In Christian theology, a mandate is an order given from God that must be obeyed without question. For example, the mandate given to Abraham to offer his son Isaac as a sacrifice to God. (Genesis 22:1)
Mandate Palestine	Mandate Palestine existed while the British Mandate for Palestine, which formally began in September 1923 and terminated in May 1948, was in effect. It consisted of the part of the Mandate territory to the west of a line which, in the north, followed the Jordan River. In 1917, during the First World War, Britain defeated the Ottoman Turkish forces and occupied and set up a military administration in Palestine and Syria.
Palestine	Palestine (Greek: Παλαιστ?νη, Palaistine; Latin: Palaestina; Hebrew: ????????? Eretz-Yisra'el, (formerly also ????????, Palestina); Arabic: ??????? Filas?in, Falas?in, Filis?in) is a conventional name used, among others, to describe a geographic region between the Mediterranean Sea and the Jordan River, and various adjoining lands. Other terms for the same area include Canaan, Zion, the Land of Israel, and the Holy Land. Southern Levant is another purely geographic term, often implemented for the region, which does not have political or theologic implications.

Chapter 4. PALESTINE BETWEEN THE WARS

Politics	Aristotle's Politics is a work of political philosophy. The end of the Nicomachean Ethics declared that the inquiry into ethics necessarily follows into politics, and the two works are frequently considered to be parts of a larger treatise, or perhaps connected lectures, dealing with the "philosophy of human affairs." The title of the Politics literally means "the things concerning the polis." Composition The literary character of the Politics is subject to some dispute, growing out of the textual difficulties that attended the loss of Aristotle's works. Book III ends with a sentence that is repeated almost verbatim at the start of Book VII, while the intervening Books IV-VI seem to have a very different flavor from the rest; Book IV seems to refer several times back to the discussion of the best regime contained in Books VII-VIII. Some editors have therefore inserted Books VII-VIII after Book III. At the same time, however, references to the "discourses on politics" that occur in the Nicomachean Ethics suggest that the treatise as a whole ought to conclude with the discussion of education that occurs in Book VIII of the Politics, although it is not certain that Aristotle is referring to the Politics here.
Arab Revolt	The Arab Revolt was initiated by the Sherif Hussein bin Ali with the aim of securing independence from the ruling Ottoman Turks and creating a single unified Arab state spanning from Aleppo in Syria to Aden in Yemen. The rise of nationalism under the Ottoman Empire goes back to 1821. Arab nationalism has its roots in the Mashriq, particularly in countries of Sham (the Levant). The political orientation of Arab nationalists in the years prior to the Great War was generally moderate.
Arabia	Arabia was a satrapy (province) of the Achaemenid Empire and later of the Sassanid Empire, by the name of Arabistan. Achaemenid Era

93

Achaemenid Arabia corresponded to the lands between Egypt and Mesopotamia, known as Arabia Petraea. According to Herodotus, the Cambyses did not subdue the Arabs when he attacked Egypt in 525 BCE. His successor Darius the Great does not mention the Arabs in the Behistun inscription from the first years of his reign, but mentions them in later texts.

Arab	The proper name Arab or "Arabian" (and cognates in other languages) has been used to translate several different but similar sounding words in ancient and classical texts which do not necessarily have the same meaning or origin. Grunebaum, in his book Classical Islam said that an approximate translation is "passerby" or "nomad". Will Durant, in The Age of Faith, said that Arab meant Arid.
Emir	Emir, ("commander" or "general", also "prince" ; also transliterated as amir, aamir or ameer) is a high title of nobility or office, used throughout the Muslim world. Emirs are usually considered high-ranking sheikhs, but in monarchical states the term is also used for princes, with "Emirate" being analogous to principality in this sense.
	While emir is the predominant spelling in English and many other languages, amir, closer to the original Arabic, is more common for its numerous compounds (e.g. admiral) and in individual names.
Husayn	Husayn is an Arabic name which is the diminutive of Hassan, meaning "good", "handsome" or "beautiful". It is commonly given as a male given name among Muslims, in honor of Husayn ibn Ali (626-680 AD). In some Persian sources the forms ?osayn, Hosayn, or Hossein is used.
Jaffa	Jaffa is an ancient port city believed to be one of the oldest in the world. Jaffa has been incorporated with Tel Aviv creating the city of Tel Aviv-Yafo, Israel.
	Etymology
	The name of the city is supposedly mentioned in Egyptian sources and the Amarna Letters as Yapu.

Chapter 4. PALESTINE BETWEEN THE WARS

Saudi Arabia	The Kingdom of Saudi Arabia, commonly known as Saudi Arabia is, in land area, the third largest Arab country and the largest country in the Middle East. It is bordered by Jordan and Iraq on the north and northeast, Kuwait, Qatar and the United Arab Emirates on the east, Oman on the southeast, and Yemen on the south. It is also connected to Bahrain by the King Fahd Causeway.
Zionism	Zionism is a Jewish political movement that, in its broadest sense, has supported the self-determination of the Jewish people in a sovereign Jewish national homeland. Since the establishment of the State of Israel, the Zionist movement continues primarily to advocate on behalf of the Jewish state and address threats to its continued existence and security. In a less common usage, the term may also refer to 1) non-political, Cultural Zionism, founded and represented most prominently by Ahad Ha'am; and 2) political support for the State of Israel by non-Jews, as in Christian Zionism.
Egypt	The Roman province of Egypt was established in 30 BC after Octavian (the future emperor Augustus) defeated his rival Mark Antony, deposed his lover Queen Cleopatra VII and annexed the Ptolemaic kingdom of Egypt to the Roman Empire. The province encompassed most of modern-day Egypt except for the Sinai Peninsula (which would later be conquered by Trajan). Aegyptus was bordered by the provinces of Creta et Cyrenaica to the West and Judaea to the East.
Germany	The Germany Pavilion is part of the World Showcase within Epcot at the Walt Disney World Resort. History The original design of the pavilion called for a boat ride along the Rhine river. It was to have focused on German folklore, in a similar manner to the Mexico and Norway rides.
Muhammad	Muhammad ibn 'Abdullah (ca. 570/571 - June 8, 632), (Monday, 12th Rabi' al-Awwal, Year 11 A.H). is considered the founder of the religion of Islam, and is regarded by Muslims as a messenger and prophet of God, the last law-bearer in a series of Islamic prophets, and, by most Muslims, the last prophet of Islam as taught by the Qur'an. Muslims thus consider him the restorer of an uncorrupted original monotheistic faith (islam) of Adam, Noah, Abraham, Moses, Jesus and other prophets.

Chapter 4. PALESTINE BETWEEN THE WARS

World	WORLD Magazine is a biweekly Christian news magazine, published in the United States of America by God's World Publications, a non-profit 501(c)(3) organization based in Asheville, North Carolina. WORLD differs from most other news magazines in that its declared perspective is one of conservative evangelical Protestantism. Its mission statement is "To report, interpret, and illustrate the news in a timely, accurate, enjoyable, and arresting fashion from a perspective committed to the Bible as the inerrant Word of God." Each issue features both U.S. and international news, cultural analysis, editorials and commentary, as well as book, music and movie reviews.
Al-Arabi	Al-Arabi is a monthly Arabic magazine that focuses mainly on the culture, literature, art, politics, society, and economics of the Arab world. The first edition was published in December 1958, seeking to propound the ideology of Pan-Arabism. The magazine encourages public participation, and makes use of photography and freelance work.
Samuel	Samuel is a leader of ancient Israel in the Books of Samuel in the Hebrew Bible. He is also known as a prophet and is mentioned in the Qur'an. His status, as viewed by rabbinical literature, is that he was the last of the Hebrew Judges and the first of the major prophets who began to prophesy inside the Land of Israel.
Mandate	In Christian theology, a mandate is an order given from God that must be obeyed without question. For example, the mandate given to Abraham to offer his son Isaac as a sacrifice to God. (Genesis 22:1)
Hebron	Hebron, is located in the southern West Bank, 30 km (19 mi) south of Jerusalem. Nestled in the Judean Mountains, it lies 930 meters (3,050 ft) above sea level. It is the largest city in the West Bank and home to around 165,000 Palestinians, and over 500 Jewish settlers concentrated in and around the old quarter.

Clam101

Chapter 4. PALESTINE BETWEEN THE WARS

Supreme Muslim Council	The Supreme Muslim Council was the highest body in charge of Muslim community affairs in Mandate Palestine under British control. It was established to create an advisory body composed of Muslims and Christians with whom the High Commissioner could consult. The Muslim leaders, however, sought to create an independent council to supervise the religious affairs of its community, especially in matters relating to religious trusts (waqf) and shariah courts.
Al-Karmil	Al-Karmil was a weekly Arabic language newspaper founded toward the end of Ottoman imperial rule in Palestine. Named for Mount Carmel in the Haifa district, the first issue was published in December 1908, with the stated purpose of "opposing Zionist colonization". The owner, editor and key writer for the newspaper was Najib Nassar, a Palestinian Christian and staunch anti-Zionist, whose editorials warning of the dangers posed by Zionism to the Palestinian people were often reprinted in other Syrian newspapers.
Barak	Barak, Al-Buraq the son of Abinoam from Kedesh in Naphtali, was a military general in the Book of Judges in the Bible. He was the commander of the army of Deborah, the prophetess and heroine of the Hebrew Bible. Barak and Deborah are credited with defeating the Canaanite armies led by Sisera, who for twenty years had oppressed the Israelites.
East Jerusalem	East Jerusalem refers to the parts of Jerusalem captured by Jordan in the 1948 Arab-Israeli War and then taken by Israel in the 1967 Six-Day War. It includes Jerusalem's Old City and some of the holiest sites of Judaism, Christianity, and Islam, such as the Temple Mount, Western Wall, Al-Aqsa Mosque, and the Church of the Holy Sepulchre. The term "East Jerusalem" may refer to either the area under Jordanian rule between 1949 and 1967 which was incorporated into the municipality of Jerusalem after 1967, covering some 70 km^2 (27 sq mi), or the territory of the pre-1967 Jordanian municipality, covering 6.4 km^2 (2.5 sq mi).
Ehud	Ehud ben-Gera is described in the Biblical Book of Judges as a judge who was sent by God to deliver the Israelites from the Moabite yoke. Ehud was sent to the Moabite King Eglon on the pretext of delivering the Israelites' annual tribute. He had blacksmiths make a double-edged shortsword about eighteen inches long, useful for a stabbing thrust.

101

Chapter 4. PALESTINE BETWEEN THE WARS

Labor Zionism	Labor Zionism can be described as the major stream of the left wing of the Zionist movement. It was, for many years, the most significant tendency among Zionists and Zionist organizational structure. It saw itself as the Zionist sector of the historic Jewish labor movements of Eastern and Central Europe, eventually developing local units in most countries with sizeable Jewish populations.
Lebanon	Lebanon is a mural size painting by Nabil Kanso depicting the Lebanese Civil War in a scene invoking the spirit and character of the people in the midst of horror and violence gripping the country. Amid the scene of chaos and devastation, two central figures reach across toward each other symbolically to represent the appeal for unity in defiance of the forces of division, destruction, and terror. Description Painted in oil on linen and completed in 1983, the painting Lebanon measures 28 feet (8.5 meters) long by 10 feet (3meters) tall.
Yishuv	Yishuv, Hebrew: ??????, or the full term ????? ?????? ???? ????? Hayishuv Hayehudi b'Eretz Yisrael ("The Jewish settlement in the Land of Israel") is the term used in Hebrew referring to the body of Jewish residents in the Holy Land before the establishment of the State of Israel. The residents and new settlers were referred to collectively as "the Yishuv" or "Ha-Yishuv." The term came into use in the 1880s, when there were about 25,000 Jews living in Eretz Yisrael, and continued to be used until 1948, by which time there were about 700,000 Jews there, and is used in Hebrew even nowadays to denote the Pre-State Jewish residents in the Holy Land. A distinction is sometimes drawn between the Old Yishuv and the New Yishuv. The Old Yishuv refers to all the Jews living there before the aliyah of 1882 by the Zionist movement.
Revisionist Zionism	Revisionist Zionism is a nationalist faction within the Zionist movement. It is the founding ideology of the non-religious right in Israel, and was the chief ideological competitor to the dominant socialist Labor Zionism. Revisionism is represented primarily by the Likud Party.

Chapter 4. PALESTINE BETWEEN THE WARS

Anti-Zionism	Anti-Zionism can be opposition to various ideologies within Zionism or opposition to the Jewish state of Israel founded on that concept. Sometimes the term anti-Zionism is used to describe discrimination against Israelis and Israeli culture. The term has been used both historically and in current debates to describe various religious, moral and political points of view in opposition to these, but their diversity of motivation and expression is sufficiently different that "anti-Zionism" cannot be seen as having a single ideology or source.
State	The term state is used in various senses by Catholic theologians and spiritual writers. It may be taken to signify a profession or calling in life, as where St. Paul says, in I Corinthians 7:20: "Let every man abide in the same calling in which he was called". States are classified in the Catholic Church as the clerical state, the religious state, and the secular state; and among religious states, again, we have those of the contemplative, the active, and the mixed orders.
Western	Western is a Franco-Belgian one shot comic written by Jean Van Hamme, illustrated by Grzegorz Rosinski and published by Le Lombard in French and Cinebook in English. Story Volume - Western - May 2001 ISBN 2-80361-662-9 Translations Cinebook Ltd plans to publish Western in June 2011
Western Wall	The Western Wall, Wailing Wall or Kotel ; is located in the Old City of Jerusalem at the foot of the western side of the Temple Mount. It is a remnant of the ancient wall that surrounded the Jewish Temple's courtyard and is one of the most sacred sites in Judaism outside of the Temple Mount itself. Just over half the wall, including its 17 courses located below street level, dates from the end of the Second Temple period, being constructed around 19 BCE by Herod the Great.

Prophet	In religion, a prophet is an individual who is claimed to have been contacted by the supernatural or the divine, and serves as an intermediary with humanity, delivering this newfound knowledge from the supernatural entity to other people. The message that the prophet conveys is called a prophecy. Claims of prophets have existed in many cultures through history, including Judaism, Christianity, Islam, the Sybilline and the Pythia, known as the Oracle of Delphi, in Ancient Greece, Zoroaster, the Völuspá in Old Norse and many others.
Italy	The Italy Pavilion is a part of the World Showcase within Epcot at the Walt Disney World Resort. Layout The Italian Pavilion features a plaza surrounded by a collection of buildings evocative of Venetian, Florentine, and Roman architecture. Venetian architecture is represented by a re-creation of St Mark's Campanile (bell tower) and a replica of the Doge's Palace.
Anwar	Anwar is the English transliteration of two Arabic names commonly used in the Muslim world: the male given name Anwar meaning "luminous" or the female given name Anwar (??????????), meaning "a collection of lights." Both names may also be encountered as surnames. In francophone countries, both names are usually transliterated as Anouar. The name is transliterated in Albania, Bosnia and Turkey as Enver.
Mubarak	Mubarak is an Arabic given name, which has the meaning "blessed one". A variant form is Barak or Barack, not to be confused with the unrelated Hebrew name Baraq; also anglicized as "Barak" or "Barack"). Mubarak and Barack are thus the Arabic equivalent in meaning of the Latinate "Benedict" .

Chapter 4. PALESTINE BETWEEN THE WARS

Passfield white paper	The Passfield White Paper, issued October 1, 1930, by colonial secretary Lord Passfield, was a formal statement of British policy in Palestine, which previously had been set by the Churchill White Paper of 1922. The new statement resulted from the Hope-Simpson Commission's investigation into the deeper causes of the 1929 Palestine riots, that initially started over access to the Wailing Wall. The white paper limited official Jewish immigration to a much greater degree. The paper's tone was decidedly anti-Zionist since several of its institutions were severely criticized, including the Histadrut (General Federation of Labor) and the Jewish Agency, which both promoted Jewish employment of only Jewish labor.
Al-Islah	Al-Islah, is a political party in Yemen that is absent from the Yemeni parliament. According to Al Jazeera, its ideology is partly based on Islamism. One of its main leaders is Tawakel Karman, who is also a member of parliament for the similarly named Al-Islah party that has 46 parliamentary seats.
Reform Party	The Reform Party was established by Husayin al-Khalidi in Palestine on 23 June 1935.
State	The term state is used in various senses by Catholic theologians and spiritual writers. It may be taken to signify a profession or calling in life, as where St. Paul says, in I Corinthians 7:20: "Let every man abide in the same calling in which he was called". States are classified in the Catholic Church as the clerical state, the religious state, and the secular state; and among religious states, again, we have those of the contemplative, the active, and the mixed orders.
Arab Higher Committee	The Arab Higher Committee was the central political organ of the Arab community of Mandate Palestine. It was established on 25 April 1936, on the initiative of Hajj Amin al-Husayni, the mufti of Jerusalem, and comprised the leaders of Palestinian Arab clans under the mufti's chairmanship. History The Higher Arab Committee was formed after the start of the 1936-39 Arab revolt.

Chapter 4. PALESTINE BETWEEN THE WARS

Kamil	Kamil is a Polish, Czech, and Slovak given name, equivalent to the Italian Camillo, Spanish Camilo and French Camille, deriving from Camillus, a Roman family name, which is sometimes claimed to mean "attendant at a religious service" in Latin, but may actually be of unknown Etruscan origin. The female version is Kamila, equivalent to English Camilla. Kamil is also an Arabic name which can be translated as "Perfect" or "the Perfect One".
Al-Qadir	Al-Qadir was the Abbasid Caliph in Baghdad from 991 to 1031. Grandson of al-Muqtadir, he was chosen in place of the deposed Caliph, at-Ta?i, his cousin. Banished from the Capital earlier, he was now recalled and appointed to the office he had long desired. He held the Caliphate for 40 years.
Aqaba	Aqaba is a coastal town in the far south of Jordan. It is the capital of Aqaba Governorate. Aqaba is strategically important to Jordan as it is the country's only seaport.

CRM101

Chapter 4. PALESTINE BETWEEN THE WARS

Fawzi	Fawzi may refer to: • Ali Fawzi Rebaine , the leader of the Ahd 54 political party in Algeria • Fawzi Al Shammari , a Kuwaiti athlete who competes in the 200 and 400 metres • Fawzi al-Ghazzi (1891-1929), a Syrian politician known for being the father of the Syrian constitution • Fawzi al-Mulki (1910-1962), a Jordanian diplomat and politician • Fawzi al-Qawuqji (1890-1977), the field commander of the Arab Liberation Army during the 1948 Arab-Israeli War • Fawzi Bashir Doorbeen , a Omani football midfielder • Fawzi Fayez , an Emarati footballer • Fawzi Hariri , Iraq's Minister of Industry and Minerals • Fawzi Moussouni , an Algerian international football player • Fawzi Saadi , an Algerian football player • Fawzi Salloukh, the current Foreign Minister of Lebanon • Fawzi Selu (1905-1972), a Syrian military leader, politician and head of state • Hussam Fawzi an Iraqi footballer, former captain of the Iraq national football team • Mahmoud Fawzi an Egyptian diplomat and political figure • Mohamed Fawzi an Egyptian composer and singer • Mohamed Fawzi , an Emirati football player • Mohamed Fawzi Abdalla, a football player from the United Arab Emirates (UAE) • Sinan Fawzi an Iraqi football midfielder .
Hama	Hama is a city on the banks of the Orontes River in central Syria north of Damascus. It is the provincial capital of the Hama Governorate. The city is the location of the historical city Hamath.
Peel Commission	The Peel Commission of 1936-1937, formally known as the Palestine Royal Commission, was a British Royal Commission of Inquiry set out to propose changes to the British Mandate of Palestine following the outbreak of the 1936-1939 Arab revolt in Palestine. It was headed by the Earl Peel. On 11 November, 1936, the commission arrived in Palestine to investigate the reasons behind the uprising.

Chapter 4. PALESTINE BETWEEN THE WARS

Transjordan	The Transjordan is a section of the land of Israel mentioned in the Hebrew Bible. It is the land east of the Jordan River in which the tribes of Reuben and Gad, and half the tribe of Manasseh settle. Name The prefix trans- is Latin and means "across" or beyond, and so "Transjordan" refers to the land on the other side of the Jordan River.
Response	A response is the second half of one of a set of preces, the said or sung answer by the congregation or choir to a versicle said or sung by an officiant or cantor. In the following opening of the Anglican service of Evening Prayer according to the Book of Common Prayer (BCP), the first line is the versicle and the second is the response. In some liturgical books (such as hymnals or breviaries) the symbol "R/" or "?" is used to denote a response.
Abdullah	Abdullah is a common Arabic male name. Humility before Allah is an essential value of Islam, hence Abdullah is a favorite name among Muslims. It was once common among Arabic-speaking Jews as well, especially Iraqi Jews.
Alexander	Alexander, son of Perseus of Macedon, was a child at the conquest of his father by the Romans, and after the triumph of Aemilus Paullus in 167 BC, was kept in custody at Alba Fucens, together with his father. He became skilful in the toreutic art, learned the Latin language, and became a public notary.
Galilee	Galilee, is a large region in northern Israel which overlaps with much of the administrative North District of the country. Traditionally divided into Upper Galilee, Lower Galilee, and Western Galilee, extending from Dan to the north, at the base of Mount Hermon, along Mount Lebanon to the ridges of Mount Carmel and Mount Gilboa to the south, and from the Jordan Rift Valley to the east across the plains of the Jezreel Valley and Acre to the shores of the Mediterranean Sea and the Coastal Plain in the west.

Chapter 4. PALESTINE BETWEEN THE WARS

	Most of Galilee consists of rocky terrain, at heights of between 500 and 700 metres.
Hajj	The Hajj is the annual pilgrimage to Mecca, Saudi Arabia. It is one of the largest annual pilgrimages in the world, and is the fifth pillar of Islam, a religious duty that must be carried out at least once in their lifetime by every able-bodied Muslim who can afford to do so. The Hajj is a demonstration of the solidarity of the Muslim people, and their submission to God .
Judea	35°18′23″E? / ?31.69889°N 35.30639°E Judea, when Roman Judea was renamed Syria Palaestina following the Jewish Bar Kokhba revolt. Etymology The name Judea is a Greek and Roman adaptation of the name "Judah", which originally encompassed the territory of the Israelite tribe of that name and later of the ancient Kingdom of Judah. It was the name in use in English throughout history until the Jordanian occupation of the area.
Samaria	Samaria is a term used for a mountainous region roughly corresponding to the northern part of the West Bank. According to 1 Kings 16:24, it is derived from the individual [or clan] Shemer, from whom Omri purchased the site. The name was the only name used for this area from ancient times until the Jordanian conquest of 1948, at which point the Jordanian occupiers coined the term West Bank.
Sharif	Sharif or Chérif is a traditional Arab tribal title given to those who serve as the protector of the tribe and all tribal assets, such as property, wells, and land. In origin, the word is an adjective meaning "noble", "highborn". The feminine singular is sharifa(h) (.
West Bank	The West Bank of the Jordan River is the landlocked geographical eastern part of the Palestinian territories located in the Western Asia. To the west, north, and south, the West Bank shares borders with the state of Israel. To the east, across the Jordan River, lies the Hashemite Kingdom of Jordan.

Chapter 4. PALESTINE BETWEEN THE WARS

Alliance	This article incorporates text from Easton's Bible Dictionary (1897), a publication now in the public domain. Abraham formed an alliance with some of the Canaanitish princes (Gen. 14:13), also with Abimelech (21:22-32). Joshua and the elders of Israel entered into an alliance with the Gibeonites (Josh. 9:3-27). When the Israelites entered Canaan they were forbidden to enter into alliances with the inhabitants of the country (Lev. 18:3, 4; 20:22, 23).
Baghdad	Baghdad is the capital of Iraq, as well as the coterminous Baghdad Governorate. With an estimated population between 7 and 7.5 million, it is the largest city in Iraq, the second largest city in the Arab World (after Cairo, Egypt), and the second largest city in Western Asia (after Tehran, Iran). Located along the Tigris River, the city was founded in the 8th century and became the capital of the Abbasid Caliphate.
Irgun	Irgun was a Zionist paramilitary group that operated in the British mandate of Palestine between 1931 and 1948. It was an offshoot of the earlier and larger Jewish paramilitary organization Haganah . Since the group originally broke from the Haganah it became known as the Haganah Bet, or alternatively as Haganah Ha'leumit (????? ???????) or Ha'ma'amad (??????). Irgun members were absorbed into the Israel Defence Forces at the start of the 1948 Arab-Israeli war.
Kuwait	The State of Kuwait is a sovereign Arab nation situated in the northeast of the Arabian Peninsula in Western Asia. It is bordered by Saudi Arabia to the south, and Iraq to the north. It lies on the northwestern shore of the Persian Gulf.
Nuri	Nuri is a place in modern Sudan on the south (east) side of the Nile. Close to it, there are pyramids belonging to Nubian kings. Nuri is situated about 15 km north of Sanam, and 10 km from Jebel Barkal.
Arab world	The Arab world refers to Arabic-speaking countries stretching from the Atlantic Ocean in the west to the Arabian Sea in the east, and from the Mediterranean Sea in the north to the Horn of Africa and the Indian Ocean in the southeast.

Chapter 4. PALESTINE BETWEEN THE WARS

Chapter 4. PALESTINE BETWEEN THE WARS

It consists of 22 countries and territories with a combined population of 360 million people straddling North Africa and Western Asia.

The sentiment of Arab nationalism arose in the second half of the 19th century along with other nationalisms within the failing Ottoman Empire.

Iraq	Iraq ; officially the Republic of Iraq is a country in Western Asia spanning most of the northwestern end of the Zagros mountain range, the eastern part of the Syrian Desert and the northern part of the Arabian Desert.

Iraq is bordered by Jordan to the west, Syria to the northwest, Turkey to the north, Iran to the east, and Kuwait and Saudi Arabia to the south. Iraq has a narrow section of coastline measuring 58 km (35 miles) on the northern Persian Gulf.

Correspondence	In theology, correspondence is the relationship between spiritual and natural realities, or between mental and physical realities. The term was coined by the 18th century theologian Emanuel Swedenborg in his Arcana Coelestia (1749-1756) and Heaven and Hell (1758) and other works.

Swedenborg states that there is a correspondence between, for example: thought and speech, between intention and action, between mind and body, and between God and creation.

Catholic	The word catholic comes from the Greek phrase καθ?λου (kath'holou), meaning "on the whole," "according to the whole" or "in general", and is a combination of the Greek words κατ? meaning "about" and ?λος meaning "whole". The word in English can mean either "including a wide variety of things; all-embracing" or "of the Roman Catholic faith." as "relating to the historic doctrine and practice of the Western Church." It was first used to describe the Christian Church in the early 2nd century to emphasize its universal scope. In the context of Christian ecclesiology, it has a rich history and several usages.
Germany	The Germany Pavilion is part of the World Showcase within Epcot at the Walt Disney World Resort. History The original design of the pavilion called for a boat ride along the Rhine river. It was to have focused on German folklore, in a similar manner to the Mexico and Norway rides.
Lebanon	Lebanon is a mural size painting by Nabil Kanso depicting the Lebanese Civil War in a scene invoking the spirit and character of the people in the midst of horror and violence gripping the country. Amid the scene of chaos and devastation, two central figures reach across toward each other symbolically to represent the appeal for unity in defiance of the forces of division, destruction, and terror. Description Painted in oil on linen and completed in 1983, the painting Lebanon measures 28 feet (8.5 meters) long by 10 feet (3meters) tall.
Ottoman Empire	The Ottoman Empire was an empire that lasted from 27 July 1299 to 29 October 1923.

At the height of its power, in the 16th and 17th centuries, the empire spanned three continents, controlling much of Southeastern Europe, Western Asia and North Africa. The Ottoman Empire contained 29 provinces and numerous vassal states, some of which were later absorbed into the empire, while others were granted various types of autonomy during the course of centuries. The empire also temporarily gained authority over distant overseas lands through declarations of allegiance to the Ottoman Sultan and Caliph, such as the declaration by the Sultan of Aceh in 1565; or through the temporary acquisitions of islands in the Atlantic Ocean, such as Lanzarote in 1585.

World

WORLD Magazine is a biweekly Christian news magazine, published in the United States of America by God's World Publications, a non-profit 501(c)(3) organization based in Asheville, North Carolina. WORLD differs from most other news magazines in that its declared perspective is one of conservative evangelical Protestantism. Its mission statement is "To report, interpret, and illustrate the news in a timely, accurate, enjoyable, and arresting fashion from a perspective committed to the Bible as the inerrant Word of God."

Each issue features both U.S. and international news, cultural analysis, editorials and commentary, as well as book, music and movie reviews.

Allies

Allies is a Christian rock band. They released six albums during the 1980s and early 1990s.

Band members

The most notable band members were guitarist Randy Thomas, formerly of the Jesus music group Sweet Comfort Band and vocalist Bob Carlisle.

Cold War

Cold War is a video game developed by Czech developer Mindware Studios and published by DreamCatcher Games (Linux Game Publishing for Linux). The game is similar to the Splinter Cell series of games in that it uses a stealth-action system of gameplay. The game distinguishes itself by adding an invention system where the player can use seemingly useless objects to create tools and weapons.

125

Chapter 5. WORLD WAR II AND THE CREATION OF THE STATE OF ISRAEL, 1939-1949

Palestine	Palestine (Greek: Παλαιστ?νη, Palaistine; Latin: Palaestina; Hebrew: ????????? Eretz-Yisra'el, (formerly also ????????, Palestina); Arabic: ??????? Filas?in, Falas?in, Filis?in) is a conventional name used, among others, to describe a geographic region between the Mediterranean Sea and the Jordan River, and various adjoining lands.

Other terms for the same area include Canaan, Zion, the Land of Israel, and the Holy Land. Southern Levant is another purely geographic term, often implemented for the region, which does not have political or theologic implications. |
| Prime | Prime, is a fixed time of prayer of the traditional Divine Office (Canonical Hours), said at the first hour of daylight (approximately 6:00 a.m)., between the morning Hour of Lauds and the 9 a.m. Hour of Terce. It is part of the Christian liturgies of Eastern Christianity, but in the Latin Rite it was suppressed by the Second Vatican Council. However, clergy who have an obligation to celebrate the Liturgy of the Hours may still fulfil their obligation by using the Roman Breviary promulgated by Pope John XXIII in 1962, which contains the Hour of Prime. |
| State | The term state is used in various senses by Catholic theologians and spiritual writers.

It may be taken to signify a profession or calling in life, as where St. Paul says, in I Corinthians 7:20: "Let every man abide in the same calling in which he was called". States are classified in the Catholic Church as the clerical state, the religious state, and the secular state; and among religious states, again, we have those of the contemplative, the active, and the mixed orders. |
| Hajj | The Hajj is the annual pilgrimage to Mecca, Saudi Arabia. It is one of the largest annual pilgrimages in the world, and is the fifth pillar of Islam, a religious duty that must be carried out at least once in their lifetime by every able-bodied Muslim who can afford to do so. The Hajj is a demonstration of the solidarity of the Muslim people, and their submission to God . |
| Hama | Hama is a city on the banks of the Orontes River in central Syria north of Damascus. It is the provincial capital of the Hama Governorate. The city is the location of the historical city Hamath. |

127

Chapter 5. WORLD WAR II AND THE CREATION OF THE STATE OF ISRAEL, 1939-1949

Zionism	Zionism is a Jewish political movement that, in its broadest sense, has supported the self-determination of the Jewish people in a sovereign Jewish national homeland. Since the establishment of the State of Israel, the Zionist movement continues primarily to advocate on behalf of the Jewish state and address threats to its continued existence and security. In a less common usage, the term may also refer to 1) non-political, Cultural Zionism, founded and represented most prominently by Ahad Ha'am; and 2) political support for the State of Israel by non-Jews, as in Christian Zionism.
Politics	Aristotle's Politics is a work of political philosophy. The end of the Nicomachean Ethics declared that the inquiry into ethics necessarily follows into politics, and the two works are frequently considered to be parts of a larger treatise, or perhaps connected lectures, dealing with the "philosophy of human affairs." The title of the Politics literally means "the things concerning the polis." Composition The literary character of the Politics is subject to some dispute, growing out of the textual difficulties that attended the loss of Aristotle's works. Book III ends with a sentence that is repeated almost verbatim at the start of Book VII, while the intervening Books IV-VI seem to have a very different flavor from the rest; Book IV seems to refer several times back to the discussion of the best regime contained in Books VII-VIII. Some editors have therefore inserted Books VII-VIII after Book III. At the same time, however, references to the "discourses on politics" that occur in the Nicomachean Ethics suggest that the treatise as a whole ought to conclude with the discussion of education that occurs in Book VIII of the Politics, although it is not certain that Aristotle is referring to the Politics here.
Alexander	Alexander, son of Perseus of Macedon, was a child at the conquest of his father by the Romans, and after the triumph of Aemilus Paullus in 167 BC, was kept in custody at Alba Fucens, together with his father. He became skilful in the toreutic art, learned the Latin language, and became a public notary.
Assassination	An assassination is "to murder (a usually prominent person) by a sudden and/or secret attack, often for political reasons." An additional definition is "the act of deliberately killing someone especially a public figure, usually for hire or for political reasons."

Assassinations may be prompted by religious, ideological, political, or military motives. Additionally, assassins may be prompted by financial gain, revenge for perceived grievances, a desire to acquire fame or notoriety (that is, a psychological need to garner personal public recognition), a wish to form some kind of "relationship" with the public figure, a wish or at least willingness to be killed or commit suicide in the attack.

Etymology

The word assassin is derived from the word Hashshashin, and shares its etymological roots with hashish .

Biltmore Conference	The Biltmore Conference, also known by its resolution as the Biltmore Program, was a fundamental departure from traditional Zionist policy with its demand "that Palestine be established as a Jewish Commonwealth." The meeting was held in New York City at the prestigious Biltmore Hotel from May 6 to May 11, 1942 with 600 delegates and Zionist leaders from 18 countries attending.

Prior to Biltmore, official Zionism steadfastly refused to formulate the ultimate aim of the movement preferring instead to concentrate on the practical task of building the Jewish National Home. The Biltmore Program became the official Zionist stand on the ultimate aim of the movement. |
| Egypt | The Roman province of Egypt was established in 30 BC after Octavian (the future emperor Augustus) defeated his rival Mark Antony, deposed his lover Queen Cleopatra VII and annexed the Ptolemaic kingdom of Egypt to the Roman Empire. The province encompassed most of modern-day Egypt except for the Sinai Peninsula (which would later be conquered by Trajan). Aegyptus was bordered by the provinces of Creta et Cyrenaica to the West and Judaea to the East. |
| Aswan | Aswan, formerly spelled Assuan, is a city in the south of Egypt, the capital of the Aswan Governorate. |

	It stands on the east bank of the Nile at the first cataract and is a busy market and tourist centre. The modern city has expanded and includes the formerly separate community on the island of Elephantine.
Aswan Dam	The Aswan Dam is an embankment dam situated across the Nile River in Aswan, Egypt. Since the 1950s, the name commonly refers to the High Dam, which is larger and newer than the Aswan Low Dam, which was first completed in 1902. Following Egypt's independence from the United Kingdom, the High Dam was constructed between 1960 and 1970. It aimed to increase economic production by further regulating the annual river flooding and providing storage of water for agriculture, and later, to generate hydroelectricity. The dam has had a significant impact on the economy and culture of Egypt.
Suez Crisis	The Suez Crisis, also referred to as the Tripartite Aggression, was a war fought by Britain, France, and Israel against Egypt beginning on 29 October 1956. The attack followed Egypt's decision of 26 July 1956 to nationalize the Suez Canal, after the withdrawal of an offer by Britain and the United States to fund the building of the Aswan Dam, which was partly in response to Egypt recognizing the People's Republic of China during the height of tensions between China and Taiwan. Britain and France were also strongly opposed to Nasser's plan to annex the Sudan.
Arab	The proper name Arab or "Arabian" (and cognates in other languages) has been used to translate several different but similar sounding words in ancient and classical texts which do not necessarily have the same meaning or origin. Grunebaum, in his book Classical Islam said that an approximate translation is "passerby" or "nomad". Will Durant, in The Age of Faith, said that Arab meant Arid.
Baghdad	Baghdad is the capital of Iraq, as well as the coterminous Baghdad Governorate. With an estimated population between 7 and 7.5 million, it is the largest city in Iraq, the second largest city in the Arab World (after Cairo, Egypt), and the second largest city in Western Asia (after Tehran, Iran).

Cram101

	Located along the Tigris River, the city was founded in the 8th century and became the capital of the Abbasid Caliphate.
Husayn	Husayn is an Arabic name which is the diminutive of Hassan, meaning "good", "handsome" or "beautiful". It is commonly given as a male given name among Muslims, in honor of Husayn ibn Ali (626-680 AD). In some Persian sources the forms ?osayn, Hosayn, or Hossein is used.
Irgun	Irgun was a Zionist paramilitary group that operated in the British mandate of Palestine between 1931 and 1948. It was an offshoot of the earlier and larger Jewish paramilitary organization Haganah . Since the group originally broke from the Haganah it became known as the Haganah Bet, or alternatively as Haganah Ha'leumit (????? ???????) or Ha'ma'amad (??????). Irgun members were absorbed into the Israel Defence Forces at the start of the 1948 Arab-Israeli war.
Kuwait	The State of Kuwait is a sovereign Arab nation situated in the northeast of the Arabian Peninsula in Western Asia. It is bordered by Saudi Arabia to the south, and Iraq to the north. It lies on the northwestern shore of the Persian Gulf.
Nuri	Nuri is a place in modern Sudan on the south (east) side of the Nile. Close to it, there are pyramids belonging to Nubian kings. Nuri is situated about 15 km north of Sanam, and 10 km from Jebel Barkal.
Revisionist Zionism	Revisionist Zionism is a nationalist faction within the Zionist movement. It is the founding ideology of the non-religious right in Israel, and was the chief ideological competitor to the dominant socialist Labor Zionism. Revisionism is represented primarily by the Likud Party.
Arab Higher Committee	The Arab Higher Committee was the central political organ of the Arab community of Mandate Palestine. It was established on 25 April 1936, on the initiative of Hajj Amin al-Husayni, the mufti of Jerusalem, and comprised the leaders of Palestinian Arab clans under the mufti's chairmanship. History The Higher Arab Committee was formed after the start of the 1936-39 Arab revolt.

CTam\IOI

Chapter 5. WORLD WAR II AND THE CREATION OF THE STATE OF ISRAEL, 1939-1949

Mandate	In Christian theology, a mandate is an order given from God that must be obeyed without question. For example, the mandate given to Abraham to offer his son Isaac as a sacrifice to God. (Genesis 22:1)
Mount Lebanon	Mount Lebanon, as a geographic designation, is the Lebanese mountain range, known as the Western Mountain Range of Lebanon. It extends across the whole country along about 160 km (99 mi), parallel to the Mediterranean coast with the highest peak, Qurnat as Sawda', at 3,088 m (10,131 ft). Lebanon has historically been defined by these mountains, which provided protection for the local population.
Al-Islah	Al-Islah, is a political party in Yemen that is absent from the Yemeni parliament. According to Al Jazeera, its ideology is partly based on Islamism. One of its main leaders is Tawakel Karman, who is also a member of parliament for the similarly named Al-Islah party that has 46 parliamentary seats.
Reform Party	The Reform Party was established by Husayin al-Khalidi in Palestine on 23 June 1935.
Jerusalem	Jerusalem [ii] is the capital of Israel, though not internationally recognized as such.[iii] If the area and population of East Jerusalem is included, it is Israel's largest city in both population and area, with a population of 763,800 residents over an area of 125.1 km^2 (48.3 sq mi).[iv] Located in the Judean Mountains, between the Mediterranean Sea and the northern edge of the Dead Sea, modern Jerusalem has grown far beyond the boundaries of the Old City. Jerusalem is a holy city to the three major Abrahamic religions--Judaism, Christianity and Islam. In Judaism, Jerusalem has been the holiest city since, according to the Torah, King David of Israel first established it as the capital of the united Kingdom of Israel in c. 1000 BCE, and his son Solomon commissioned the building of the First Temple in the city.
Arab world	The Arab world refers to Arabic-speaking countries stretching from the Atlantic Ocean in the west to the Arabian Sea in the east, and from the Mediterranean Sea in the north to the Horn of Africa and the Indian Ocean in the southeast.

It consists of 22 countries and territories with a combined population of 360 million people straddling North Africa and Western Asia.

The sentiment of Arab nationalism arose in the second half of the 19th century along with other nationalisms within the failing Ottoman Empire.

Syria	Syria, officially the Syrian Arab Republic, is a country in Western Asia, bordering Lebanon and the Mediterranean Sea to the West, Turkey to the north, Iraq to the east, Jordan to the south, and Israel to the southwest. The name Syria formerly comprised the entire region of the Levant, while the modern state encompasses the site of several ancient kingdoms and empires, including the Eblan civilization of the third millennium BC. In the Islamic era, its capital city, Damascus, was the seat of the Umayyad Empire and a provincial capital of the Mamluk Empire. Damascus is one of the oldest continuously inhabited cities in the world.
Ancients	The Ancients were a group of English artists who were brought together by their attraction to archaism in art and admiration for the work of William Blake. The core members of the Ancients were Samuel Palmer, George Richmond, Edward Calvert. They met in Blake's apartment, dubbed the "House of Interpreter" and at the home of Samuel Palmer in the Kent village of Shoreham.
Arab Revolt	The Arab Revolt was initiated by the Sherif Hussein bin Ali with the aim of securing independence from the ruling Ottoman Turks and creating a single unified Arab state spanning from Aleppo in Syria to Aden in Yemen. The rise of nationalism under the Ottoman Empire goes back to 1821. Arab nationalism has its roots in the Mashriq, particularly in countries of Sham (the Levant). The political orientation of Arab nationalists in the years prior to the Great War was generally moderate.

Arabia	Arabia was a satrapy (province) of the Achaemenid Empire and later of the Sassanid Empire, by the name of Arabistan.
	Achaemenid Era
	Achaemenid Arabia corresponded to the lands between Egypt and Mesopotamia, known as Arabia Petraea. According to Herodotus, the Cambyses did not subdue the Arabs when he attacked Egypt in 525 BCE. His successor Darius the Great does not mention the Arabs in the Behistun inscription from the first years of his reign, but mentions them in later texts.
Emir	Emir, ("commander" or "general", also "prince" ; also transliterated as amir, aamir or ameer) is a high title of nobility or office, used throughout the Muslim world. Emirs are usually considered high-ranking sheikhs, but in monarchical states the term is also used for princes, with "Emirate" being analogous to principality in this sense.
	While emir is the predominant spelling in English and many other languages, amir, closer to the original Arabic, is more common for its numerous compounds (e.g. admiral) and in individual names.
Fertile Crescent	The Fertile Crescent is a region in Western Asia. It includes the comparatively fertile regions of Mesopotamia and the Levant, delimited by the dry climate of the Syrian Desert to the south and the Anatolian highlands to the north. The region is often considered the cradle of civilization, saw the development of many of the earliest human civilizations, and is the birthplace of writing and the wheel.
King David	King David is a film about the second king of Israel, David.
	It was filmed in 1985 in Matera and Craco, Italy. It was directed by Bruce Beresford and starred Richard Gere in the title role.

141

CŁam101

Chapter 5. WORLD WAR II AND THE CREATION OF THE STATE OF ISRAEL, 1939-1949

Saudi Arabia	The Kingdom of Saudi Arabia, commonly known as Saudi Arabia is, in land area, the third largest Arab country and the largest country in the Middle East. It is bordered by Jordan and Iraq on the north and northeast, Kuwait, Qatar and the United Arab Emirates on the east, Oman on the southeast, and Yemen on the south. It is also connected to Bahrain by the King Fahd Causeway.
Hebron	Hebron, is located in the southern West Bank, 30 km (19 mi) south of Jerusalem. Nestled in the Judean Mountains, it lies 930 meters (3,050 ft) above sea level. It is the largest city in the West Bank and home to around 165,000 Palestinians, and over 500 Jewish settlers concentrated in and around the old quarter.
India	India was an ecclesiastical province of the Church of the East, at least nominally, from the seventh to the sixteenth century. The Malabar Coast of India had long been home to a thriving East Syrian (Nestorian) Christian community, known as the St. Thomas Christians. The community traces its origins to the evangelical activity of Thomas the Apostle in the 1st century.
Difference	Difference is a key concept of continental philosophy, opposed to Identity. Gilles Deleuze's Difference and Repetition (1968) was an attempt, to think Difference as having an ontological privilege over Identity, inversing the traditional relationship between those two concepts.
East Jerusalem	East Jerusalem refers to the parts of Jerusalem captured by Jordan in the 1948 Arab-Israeli War and then taken by Israel in the 1967 Six-Day War. It includes Jerusalem's Old City and some of the holiest sites of Judaism, Christianity, and Islam, such as the Temple Mount, Western Wall, Al-Aqsa Mosque, and the Church of the Holy Sepulchre. The term "East Jerusalem" may refer to either the area under Jordanian rule between 1949 and 1967 which was incorporated into the municipality of Jerusalem after 1967, covering some 70 km^2 (27 sq mi), or the territory of the pre-1967 Jordanian municipality, covering 6.4 km^2 (2.5 sq mi).
Response	A response is the second half of one of a set of preces, the said or sung answer by the congregation or choir to a versicle said or sung by an officiant or cantor. In the following opening of the Anglican service of Evening Prayer according to the Book of Common Prayer (BCP), the first line is the versicle and the second is the response.

Chapter 5. WORLD WAR II AND THE CREATION OF THE STATE OF ISRAEL, 1939-1949

	In some liturgical books (such as hymnals or breviaries) the symbol "R/" or "?" is used to denote a response.
Mandate Palestine	Mandate Palestine existed while the British Mandate for Palestine, which formally began in September 1923 and terminated in May 1948, was in effect. It consisted of the part of the Mandate territory to the west of a line which, in the north, followed the Jordan River.
	In 1917, during the First World War, Britain defeated the Ottoman Turkish forces and occupied and set up a military administration in Palestine and Syria.
Yishuv	Yishuv, Hebrew: ??????, or the full term ????? ?????? ???? ????? Hayishuv Hayehudi b'Eretz Yisrael ("The Jewish settlement in the Land of Israel") is the term used in Hebrew referring to the body of Jewish residents in the Holy Land before the establishment of the State of Israel. The residents and new settlers were referred to collectively as "the Yishuv" or "Ha-Yishuv." The term came into use in the 1880s, when there were about 25,000 Jews living in Eretz Yisrael, and continued to be used until 1948, by which time there were about 700,000 Jews there, and is used in Hebrew even nowadays to denote the Pre-State Jewish residents in the Holy Land.
	A distinction is sometimes drawn between the Old Yishuv and the New Yishuv.
	The Old Yishuv refers to all the Jews living there before the aliyah of 1882 by the Zionist movement.
Abbas	Abbas means "lion" in Arabic. (Austere: (1) severely simple in appearance. (2) strict, stern).
Abdullah	Abdullah is a common Arabic male name. Humility before Allah is an essential value of Islam, hence Abdullah is a favorite name among Muslims. It was once common among Arabic-speaking Jews as well, especially Iraqi Jews.

Chapter 5. WORLD WAR II AND THE CREATION OF THE STATE OF ISRAEL, 1939-1949

Kamil	Kamil is a Polish, Czech, and Slovak given name, equivalent to the Italian Camillo, Spanish Camilo and French Camille, deriving from Camillus, a Roman family name, which is sometimes claimed to mean "attendant at a religious service" in Latin, but may actually be of unknown Etruscan origin. The female version is Kamila, equivalent to English Camilla. Kamil is also an Arabic name which can be translated as "Perfect" or "the Perfect One".
Sharif	Sharif or Chérif is a traditional Arab tribal title given to those who serve as the protector of the tribe and all tribal assets, such as property, wells, and land. In origin, the word is an adjective meaning "noble", "highborn". The feminine singular is sharifa(h) (.
Transjordan	The Transjordan is a section of the land of Israel mentioned in the Hebrew Bible. It is the land east of the Jordan River in which the tribes of Reuben and Gad, and half the tribe of Manasseh settle. Name The prefix trans- is Latin and means "across" or beyond, and so "Transjordan" refers to the land on the other side of the Jordan River.
Al-Qadir	Al-Qadir was the Abbasid Caliph in Baghdad from 991 to 1031. Grandson of al-Muqtadir, he was chosen in place of the deposed Caliph, at-Ta?i, his cousin. Banished from the Capital earlier, he was now recalled and appointed to the office he had long desired. He held the Caliphate for 40 years.
Alliance	This article incorporates text from Easton's Bible Dictionary (1897), a publication now in the public domain. Abraham formed an alliance with some of the Canaanitish princes (Gen. 14:13), also with Abimelech (21:22-32). Joshua and the elders of Israel entered into an alliance with the Gibeonites (Josh. 9:3-27). When the Israelites entered Canaan they were forbidden to enter into alliances with the inhabitants of the country (Lev. 18:3, 4; 20:22, 23).

Chapter 5. WORLD WAR II AND THE CREATION OF THE STATE OF ISRAEL, 1939-1949

Jaffa	Jaffa is an ancient port city believed to be one of the oldest in the world. Jaffa has been incorporated with Tel Aviv creating the city of Tel Aviv-Yafo, Israel. Etymology The name of the city is supposedly mentioned in Egyptian sources and the Amarna Letters as Yapu.
West Bank	The West Bank of the Jordan River is the landlocked geographical eastern part of the Palestinian territories located in the Western Asia. To the west, north, and south, the West Bank shares borders with the state of Israel. To the east, across the Jordan River, lies the Hashemite Kingdom of Jordan.
Aqaba	Aqaba is a coastal town in the far south of Jordan. It is the capital of Aqaba Governorate. Aqaba is strategically important to Jordan as it is the country's only seaport.
Old City	The Old City is a 0.9 square kilometer (0.35 square mile) walled area within the modern city of Jerusalem. Until the 1860s this area constituted the entire city of Jerusalem. The Old City is home to several sites of key religious importance: the Temple Mount and its Western Wall for Jews, the Church of the Holy Sepulchre for Christians, and the Dome of the Rock and al-Aqsa Mosque for Muslims.
Galilee	Galilee, is a large region in northern Israel which overlaps with much of the administrative North District of the country. Traditionally divided into Upper Galilee, Lower Galilee, and Western Galilee, extending from Dan to the north, at the base of Mount Hermon, along Mount Lebanon to the ridges of Mount Carmel and Mount Gilboa to the south, and from the Jordan Rift Valley to the east across the plains of the Jezreel Valley and Acre to the shores of the Mediterranean Sea and the Coastal Plain in the west. Most of Galilee consists of rocky terrain, at heights of between 500 and 700 metres.

Ariel	Ariel is an Israeli settlement and a city in the central West Bank. Established in 1978, its population at the end of 2009 was 17,600, including 7,000 immigrants who came to Israel after 1990. It is the fourth largest Jewish settlement city in the West Bank., after Modi'in Illit, Beitar Illit, and Ma'ale Adumim.
	In Hebrew, Ariel, literally means 'Lion of God'.

Clam101

Chapter 6. THE BEGINNING OF THE ARAB-ISRAELI CONFLICT: The Search for Security, 1949-1957

Aqaba	Aqaba is a coastal town in the far south of Jordan. It is the capital of Aqaba Governorate. Aqaba is strategically important to Jordan as it is the country's only seaport.
Arab	The proper name Arab or "Arabian" (and cognates in other languages) has been used to translate several different but similar sounding words in ancient and classical texts which do not necessarily have the same meaning or origin. Grunebaum, in his book Classical Islam said that an approximate translation is "passerby" or "nomad". Will Durant, in The Age of Faith, said that Arab meant Arid.
Egypt	The Roman province of Egypt was established in 30 BC after Octavian (the future emperor Augustus) defeated his rival Mark Antony, deposed his lover Queen Cleopatra VII and annexed the Ptolemaic kingdom of Egypt to the Roman Empire. The province encompassed most of modern-day Egypt except for the Sinai Peninsula (which would later be conquered by Trajan). Aegyptus was bordered by the provinces of Creta et Cyrenaica to the West and Judaea to the East.
Zionism	Zionism is a Jewish political movement that, in its broadest sense, has supported the self-determination of the Jewish people in a sovereign Jewish national homeland. Since the establishment of the State of Israel, the Zionist movement continues primarily to advocate on behalf of the Jewish state and address threats to its continued existence and security. In a less common usage, the term may also refer to 1) non-political, Cultural Zionism, founded and represented most prominently by Ahad Ha'am; and 2) political support for the State of Israel by non-Jews, as in Christian Zionism.
State	The term state is used in various senses by Catholic theologians and spiritual writers. It may be taken to signify a profession or calling in life, as where St. Paul says, in I Corinthians 7:20: "Let every man abide in the same calling in which he was called". States are classified in the Catholic Church as the clerical state, the religious state, and the secular state; and among religious states, again, we have those of the contemplative, the active, and the mixed orders.
Baghdad	Baghdad is the capital of Iraq, as well as the coterminous Baghdad Governorate. With an estimated population between 7 and 7.5 million, it is the largest city in Iraq, the second largest city in the Arab World (after Cairo, Egypt), and the second largest city in Western Asia (after Tehran, Iran).

	Located along the Tigris River, the city was founded in the 8th century and became the capital of the Abbasid Caliphate.
Cold War	Cold War is a video game developed by Czech developer Mindware Studios and published by DreamCatcher Games (Linux Game Publishing for Linux). The game is similar to the Splinter Cell series of games in that it uses a stealth-action system of gameplay. The game distinguishes itself by adding an invention system where the player can use seemingly useless objects to create tools and weapons.
Hebron	Hebron, is located in the southern West Bank, 30 km (19 mi) south of Jerusalem. Nestled in the Judean Mountains, it lies 930 meters (3,050 ft) above sea level. It is the largest city in the West Bank and home to around 165,000 Palestinians, and over 500 Jewish settlers concentrated in and around the old quarter.
Lebanon	Lebanon is a mural size painting by Nabil Kanso depicting the Lebanese Civil War in a scene invoking the spirit and character of the people in the midst of horror and violence gripping the country. Amid the scene of chaos and devastation, two central figures reach across toward each other symbolically to represent the appeal for unity in defiance of the forces of division, destruction, and terror. Description Painted in oil on linen and completed in 1983, the painting Lebanon measures 28 feet (8.5 meters) long by 10 feet (3meters) tall.
Suez Crisis	The Suez Crisis, also referred to as the Tripartite Aggression, was a war fought by Britain, France, and Israel against Egypt beginning on 29 October 1956.

	The attack followed Egypt's decision of 26 July 1956 to nationalize the Suez Canal, after the withdrawal of an offer by Britain and the United States to fund the building of the Aswan Dam, which was partly in response to Egypt recognizing the People's Republic of China during the height of tensions between China and Taiwan. Britain and France were also strongly opposed to Nasser's plan to annex the Sudan.
Difference	Difference is a key concept of continental philosophy, opposed to Identity.
	Gilles Deleuze's Difference and Repetition (1968) was an attempt, to think Difference as having an ontological privilege over Identity, inversing the traditional relationship between those two concepts.
Prime	Prime, is a fixed time of prayer of the traditional Divine Office (Canonical Hours), said at the first hour of daylight (approximately 6:00 a.m)., between the morning Hour of Lauds and the 9 a.m. Hour of Terce. It is part of the Christian liturgies of Eastern Christianity, but in the Latin Rite it was suppressed by the Second Vatican Council. However, clergy who have an obligation to celebrate the Liturgy of the Hours may still fulfil their obligation by using the Roman Breviary promulgated by Pope John XXIII in 1962, which contains the Hour of Prime.
East Jerusalem	East Jerusalem refers to the parts of Jerusalem captured by Jordan in the 1948 Arab-Israeli War and then taken by Israel in the 1967 Six-Day War. It includes Jerusalem's Old City and some of the holiest sites of Judaism, Christianity, and Islam, such as the Temple Mount, Western Wall, Al-Aqsa Mosque, and the Church of the Holy Sepulchre. The term "East Jerusalem" may refer to either the area under Jordanian rule between 1949 and 1967 which was incorporated into the municipality of Jerusalem after 1967, covering some 70 km^2 (27 sq mi), or the territory of the pre-1967 Jordanian municipality, covering 6.4 km^2 (2.5 sq mi).
Husayn	Husayn is an Arabic name which is the diminutive of Hassan, meaning "good", "handsome" or "beautiful". It is commonly given as a male given name among Muslims, in honor of Husayn ibn Ali (626-680 AD). In some Persian sources the forms ?osayn, Hosayn, or Hossein is used.

Chapter 6. THE BEGINNING OF THE ARAB-ISRAELI CONFLICT: The Search for Security, 1949-1957

Irgun	Irgun was a Zionist paramilitary group that operated in the British mandate of Palestine between 1931 and 1948. It was an offshoot of the earlier and larger Jewish paramilitary organization Haganah . Since the group originally broke from the Haganah it became known as the Haganah Bet, or alternatively as Haganah Ha'leumit (????? ???????) or Ha'ma'amad (??????). Irgun members were absorbed into the Israel Defence Forces at the start of the 1948 Arab-Israeli war.
Israeli settlement	An Israeli settlement is an Israeli civilian community on land that was captured by Israel during the Six-Day War and is considered by the international community (excluding Israel) to be occupied territory. Such settlements currently exist in the West Bank, East Jerusalem, and the Golan Heights. The International Court of Justice and the international community say these settlements are illegal,.
Jerusalem	Jerusalem [ii] is the capital of Israel, though not internationally recognized as such.[iii] If the area and population of East Jerusalem is included, it is Israel's largest city in both population and area, with a population of 763,800 residents over an area of 125.1 km^2 (48.3 sq mi).[iv] Located in the Judean Mountains, between the Mediterranean Sea and the northern edge of the Dead Sea, modern Jerusalem has grown far beyond the boundaries of the Old City. Jerusalem is a holy city to the three major Abrahamic religions--Judaism, Christianity and Islam. In Judaism, Jerusalem has been the holiest city since, according to the Torah, King David of Israel first established it as the capital of the united Kingdom of Israel in c. 1000 BCE, and his son Solomon commissioned the building of the First Temple in the city.
Kuwait	The State of Kuwait is a sovereign Arab nation situated in the northeast of the Arabian Peninsula in Western Asia. It is bordered by Saudi Arabia to the south, and Iraq to the north. It lies on the northwestern shore of the Persian Gulf.
Nuri	Nuri is a place in modern Sudan on the south (east) side of the Nile. Close to it, there are pyramids belonging to Nubian kings. Nuri is situated about 15 km north of Sanam, and 10 km from Jebel Barkal.

Orthodox	Orthodox Basketball Club formerly known as Fastlink Basketball Club is a Jordanian basketball club based in Amman, Jordan. They compete in the Jordanian Basketball Federation. Tournament records WABA Champions Cup • 1999: Champions • 2001: 2nd place • 2002: 2nd place • 2004: 1st place • 2008: 2nd place • 2009: 1st place Asia Champions Cup • 1988: 5th place • 1996: 7th place • 1999: 6th place
Revisionist Zionism	Revisionist Zionism is a nationalist faction within the Zionist movement. It is the founding ideology of the non-religious right in Israel, and was the chief ideological competitor to the dominant socialist Labor Zionism. Revisionism is represented primarily by the Likud Party.
Politics	Aristotle's Politics is a work of political philosophy. The end of the Nicomachean Ethics declared that the inquiry into ethics necessarily follows into politics, and the two works are frequently considered to be parts of a larger treatise, or perhaps connected lectures, dealing with the "philosophy of human affairs." The title of the Politics literally means "the things concerning the polis." Composition

161

The literary character of the Politics is subject to some dispute, growing out of the textual difficulties that attended the loss of Aristotle's works. Book III ends with a sentence that is repeated almost verbatim at the start of Book VII, while the intervening Books IV-VI seem to have a very different flavor from the rest; Book IV seems to refer several times back to the discussion of the best regime contained in Books VII-VIII. Some editors have therefore inserted Books VII-VIII after Book III. At the same time, however, references to the "discourses on politics" that occur in the Nicomachean Ethics suggest that the treatise as a whole ought to conclude with the discussion of education that occurs in Book VIII of the Politics, although it is not certain that Aristotle is referring to the Politics here.

Laws

The Laws is Plato's last and longest dialogue. The question asked at the beginning is not "What is law?" as one would expect. That is the question of the (pseudo?)Platonic Minos.

Catholic

The word catholic comes from the Greek phrase καθ?λou (kath'holou), meaning "on the whole," "according to the whole" or "in general", and is a combination of the Greek words κατ? meaning "about" and ?λoς meaning "whole". The word in English can mean either "including a wide variety of things; all-embracing" or "of the Roman Catholic faith." as "relating to the historic doctrine and practice of the Western Church."

It was first used to describe the Christian Church in the early 2nd century to emphasize its universal scope. In the context of Christian ecclesiology, it has a rich history and several usages.

Druze

The Druze are an esoteric monotheistic religious community found primarily in Syria, Lebanon, Israel, and Jordan, which emerged during the 11th century from Ismailism and incorporated several elements of Gnosticism, Neoplatonism and other philosophies. Some Druze call themselves Ahl al-Tawhid "People of Unitarianism or Monotheism" or al-Muwa??idun "Unitarians, Monotheists."

Location

The Druze people reside primarily in Syria, Lebanon, and Israel. The Israeli Druze are mostly in Galilee (81%), around Haifa (19%), and in the Golan Heights.

Syria

Syria, officially the Syrian Arab Republic, is a country in Western Asia, bordering Lebanon and the Mediterranean Sea to the West, Turkey to the north, Iraq to the east, Jordan to the south, and Israel to the southwest.

The name Syria formerly comprised the entire region of the Levant, while the modern state encompasses the site of several ancient kingdoms and empires, including the Eblan civilization of the third millennium BC. In the Islamic era, its capital city, Damascus, was the seat of the Umayyad Empire and a provincial capital of the Mamluk Empire. Damascus is one of the oldest continuously inhabited cities in the world.

State

The term state is used in various senses by Catholic theologians and spiritual writers.

It may be taken to signify a profession or calling in life, as where St. Paul says, in I Corinthians 7:20: "Let every man abide in the same calling in which he was called". States are classified in the Catholic Church as the clerical state, the religious state, and the secular state; and among religious states, again, we have those of the contemplative, the active, and the mixed orders.

Tripartite

In Christian theology, the tripartite viewpoint holds that man is a composite of three distinct components: body, soul and spirit. It is less popular than the bipartite view, where "soul" and "spirit" are taken as different terms for the same entity.

Scriptural Basis

The two primary proof texts for this position are as follows:

1 Thessalonians 5:23

165

Proponents of the tripartite view claim that this verse spells out clearly the three components of the human, emphasized by the descriptors of "whole" and "completely." Opponents argue that spirit and soul are merely a repetition of synonyms, a common form used elsewhere in scripture to add the idea completeness.

West Bank	The West Bank of the Jordan River is the landlocked geographical eastern part of the Palestinian territories located in the Western Asia. To the west, north, and south, the West Bank shares borders with the state of Israel. To the east, across the Jordan River, lies the Hashemite Kingdom of Jordan.

Judea

35°18′23″E? / ?31.69889°N 35.30639°E

Judea, when Roman Judea was renamed Syria Palaestina following the Jewish Bar Kokhba revolt.

Etymology

The name Judea is a Greek and Roman adaptation of the name "Judah", which originally encompassed the territory of the Israelite tribe of that name and later of the ancient Kingdom of Judah. It was the name in use in English throughout history until the Jordanian occupation of the area.

Palestine

Palestine (Greek: Παλαιστ?νη, Palaistine; Latin: Palaestina; Hebrew: ????????? Eretz-Yisra'el, (formerly also ????????, Palestina); Arabic: ??????? Filas?in, Falas?in, Filis?in) is a conventional name used, among others, to describe a geographic region between the Mediterranean Sea and the Jordan River, and various adjoining lands.

Other terms for the same area include Canaan, Zion, the Land of Israel, and the Holy Land. Southern Levant is another purely geographic term, often implemented for the region, which does not have political or theologic implications.

167

Chapter 6. THE BEGINNING OF THE ARAB-ISRAELI CONFLICT: The Search for Security, 1949-1957

Samaria	Samaria is a term used for a mountainous region roughly corresponding to the northern part of the West Bank. According to 1 Kings 16:24, it is derived from the individual [or clan] Shemer, from whom Omri purchased the site. The name was the only name used for this area from ancient times until the Jordanian conquest of 1948, at which point the Jordanian occupiers coined the term West Bank.
Abdullah	Abdullah is a common Arabic male name. Humility before Allah is an essential value of Islam, hence Abdullah is a favorite name among Muslims. It was once common among Arabic-speaking Jews as well, especially Iraqi Jews.
Emir	Emir, ("commander" or "general", also "prince" ; also transliterated as amir, aamir or ameer) is a high title of nobility or office, used throughout the Muslim world. Emirs are usually considered high-ranking sheikhs, but in monarchical states the term is also used for princes, with "Emirate" being analogous to principality in this sense. While emir is the predominant spelling in English and many other languages, amir, closer to the original Arabic, is more common for its numerous compounds (e.g. admiral) and in individual names.
Sharif	Sharif or Chérif is a traditional Arab tribal title given to those who serve as the protector of the tribe and all tribal assets, such as property, wells, and land. In origin, the word is an adjective meaning "noble", "highborn". The feminine singular is sharifa(h) (.
Transjordan	The Transjordan is a section of the land of Israel mentioned in the Hebrew Bible. It is the land east of the Jordan River in which the tribes of Reuben and Gad, and half the tribe of Manasseh settle. Name The prefix trans- is Latin and means "across" or beyond, and so "Transjordan" refers to the land on the other side of the Jordan River.
Alliance	This article incorporates text from Easton's Bible Dictionary (1897), a publication now in the public domain.

169

Abraham formed an alliance with some of the Canaanitish princes (Gen. 14:13), also with Abimelech (21:22-32). Joshua and the elders of Israel entered into an alliance with the Gibeonites (Josh. 9:3-27). When the Israelites entered Canaan they were forbidden to enter into alliances with the inhabitants of the country (Lev. 18:3, 4; 20:22, 23).

Ancients	The Ancients were a group of English artists who were brought together by their attraction to archaism in art and admiration for the work of William Blake. The core members of the Ancients were Samuel Palmer, George Richmond, Edward Calvert. They met in Blake's apartment, dubbed the "House of Interpreter" and at the home of Samuel Palmer in the Kent village of Shoreham.
Assassination	An assassination is "to murder (a usually prominent person) by a sudden and/or secret attack, often for political reasons." An additional definition is "the act of deliberately killing someone especially a public figure, usually for hire or for political reasons."
	Assassinations may be prompted by religious, ideological, political, or military motives. Additionally, assassins may be prompted by financial gain, revenge for perceived grievances, a desire to acquire fame or notoriety (that is, a psychological need to garner personal public recognition), a wish to form some kind of "relationship" with the public figure, a wish or at least willingness to be killed or commit suicide in the attack.
	Etymology
	The word assassin is derived from the word Hashshashin, and shares its etymological roots with hashish .
Arab world	The Arab world refers to Arabic-speaking countries stretching from the Atlantic Ocean in the west to the Arabian Sea in the east, and from the Mediterranean Sea in the north to the Horn of Africa and the Indian Ocean in the southeast.
	It consists of 22 countries and territories with a combined population of 360 million people straddling North Africa and Western Asia.

171

Chapter 6. THE BEGINNING OF THE ARAB-ISRAELI CONFLICT: The Search for Security, 1949-1957

The sentiment of Arab nationalism arose in the second half of the 19th century along with other nationalisms within the failing Ottoman Empire.

Arabia	Arabia was a satrapy (province) of the Achaemenid Empire and later of the Sassanid Empire, by the name of Arabistan.

Achaemenid Era

Achaemenid Arabia corresponded to the lands between Egypt and Mesopotamia, known as Arabia Petraea. According to Herodotus, the Cambyses did not subdue the Arabs when he attacked Egypt in 525 BCE. His successor Darius the Great does not mention the Arabs in the Behistun inscription from the first years of his reign, but mentions them in later texts. |
| Fertile Crescent | The Fertile Crescent is a region in Western Asia. It includes the comparatively fertile regions of Mesopotamia and the Levant, delimited by the dry climate of the Syrian Desert to the south and the Anatolian highlands to the north. The region is often considered the cradle of civilization, saw the development of many of the earliest human civilizations, and is the birthplace of writing and the wheel. |
| Hama | Hama is a city on the banks of the Orontes River in central Syria north of Damascus. It is the provincial capital of the Hama Governorate. The city is the location of the historical city Hamath. |
| Hashemite | Hashemite is the Latinate version of the Arabic: ??????, transliteration: Hašimi, and traditionally refers to those belonging to the Banu Hashim, or "clan of Hashim", a clan within the larger Quraish tribe. It also refers to an Arab dynasty whose original strength stemmed from the network of tribal alliances and blood loyalties in the Hejaz region of Arabia, along the Red Sea.

History

The Hashemites trace their ancestry from Hashim ibn Abd al-Manaf (died c. 510 AD), the great-grandfather of the Islamic prophet Muhammad, although the definition today mainly refers to the descendants of the prophet's daughter, Fatimah. |

173

Iraq	Iraq ; officially the Republic of Iraq is a country in Western Asia spanning most of the northwestern end of the Zagros mountain range, the eastern part of the Syrian Desert and the northern part of the Arabian Desert. Iraq is bordered by Jordan to the west, Syria to the northwest, Turkey to the north, Iran to the east, and Kuwait and Saudi Arabia to the south. Iraq has a narrow section of coastline measuring 58 km (35 miles) on the northern Persian Gulf.
Saudi Arabia	The Kingdom of Saudi Arabia, commonly known as Saudi Arabia is, in land area, the third largest Arab country and the largest country in the Middle East. It is bordered by Jordan and Iraq on the north and northeast, Kuwait, Qatar and the United Arab Emirates on the east, Oman on the southeast, and Yemen on the south. It is also connected to Bahrain by the King Fahd Causeway.
World	WORLD Magazine is a biweekly Christian news magazine, published in the United States of America by God's World Publications, a non-profit 501(c)(3) organization based in Asheville, North Carolina. WORLD differs from most other news magazines in that its declared perspective is one of conservative evangelical Protestantism. Its mission statement is "To report, interpret, and illustrate the news in a timely, accurate, enjoyable, and arresting fashion from a perspective committed to the Bible as the inerrant Word of God." Each issue features both U.S. and international news, cultural analysis, editorials and commentary, as well as book, music and movie reviews.
Aswan	Aswan, formerly spelled Assuan, is a city in the south of Egypt, the capital of the Aswan Governorate. It stands on the east bank of the Nile at the first cataract and is a busy market and tourist centre. The modern city has expanded and includes the formerly separate community on the island of Elephantine.

175

Aswan Dam	The Aswan Dam is an embankment dam situated across the Nile River in Aswan, Egypt. Since the 1950s, the name commonly refers to the High Dam, which is larger and newer than the Aswan Low Dam, which was first completed in 1902. Following Egypt's independence from the United Kingdom, the High Dam was constructed between 1960 and 1970. It aimed to increase economic production by further regulating the annual river flooding and providing storage of water for agriculture, and later, to generate hydroelectricity. The dam has had a significant impact on the economy and culture of Egypt.
Republic	Republic is a Hungarian rock band formed in Budapest in 1989. Their style is a unique mix of Western rock music and traditional Hungarian folk music. The band is popular in its native country and among Hungarian speaking minorities elsewhere. Members The two founding members are László Bódi and Lászlo Attila Nagy.
Lavon Affair	The Lavon Affair refers to a failed Israeli covert operation, code named Operation Susannah, conducted in Egypt in the Summer of 1954. As part of the false flag operation, a group of Egyptian Jews were recruited by Israeli military intelligence for plans to plant bombs inside Egyptian, American and British-owned targets. The attacks were to be blamed on the Muslim Brotherhood, Egyptian Communists, "unspecified malcontents" or "local nationalists" with the aim of creating a climate of sufficient violence and instability to induce the British government to retain its occupying troops in Egypt's Suez Canal zone. The operation caused no casualties, except for the members of the cell who committed suicide after being captured.
Abbas	Abbas means "lion" in Arabic. (Austere: (1) severely simple in appearance. (2) strict, stern).
Correspondence	In theology, correspondence is the relationship between spiritual and natural realities, or between mental and physical realities. The term was coined by the 18th century theologian Emanuel Swedenborg in his Arcana Coelestia (1749-1756) and Heaven and Hell (1758) and other works. Swedenborg states that there is a correspondence between, for example: thought and speech, between intention and action, between mind and body, and between God and creation.

Response	A response is the second half of one of a set of preces, the said or sung answer by the congregation or choir to a versicle said or sung by an officiant or cantor. In the following opening of the Anglican service of Evening Prayer according to the Book of Common Prayer (BCP), the first line is the versicle and the second is the response. In some liturgical books (such as hymnals or breviaries) the symbol "R/" or "?" is used to denote a response.
Belli	The Belli, also designated 'Beli' or 'Belaiscos' were an ancient pre-Roman Celtiberian people that lived in the modern Spanish province of Zaragoza from the 3rd Century BC. Origins Of mixed Illyrian and Celtic origin, probably related with the Belgic Bellovaci, they migrated to Iberia around the 4th Century BC . Location Upon arrival, the Belli settled along the middle Jiloca and Huerva rivers in Zaragoza province with their territories streching up to the Guadalope and upper Turia valleys, close to their neighbours and clients, the Titii. Their early capital was Segeda (Poyo de Maya - Zaragoza; Celtiberian mint: Sekaiza), subsequently transferred to nearby Dúron de Belmonte and later offset by Bilbilis (Valdeherrera, near Calatayud - Zaragoza; Celtiberian mint: Bilbiliz).

Clam101

Chapter 7. FROM SUEZ TO THE SIX-DAY WAR, 1957-1967

Cold War	Cold War is a video game developed by Czech developer Mindware Studios and published by DreamCatcher Games (Linux Game Publishing for Linux). The game is similar to the Splinter Cell series of games in that it uses a stealth-action system of gameplay. The game distinguishes itself by adding an invention system where the player can use seemingly useless objects to create tools and weapons.
Damascus	Damascus is the capital and the second largest city of Syria as well as one of the country's 14 governorates. The Damascus Governorate is ruled by a governor appointed by the Minister of Interior. In addition to being the oldest continuously inhabited city in the world, Damascus is a major cultural and religious center of the Levant.
Egypt	The Roman province of Egypt was established in 30 BC after Octavian (the future emperor Augustus) defeated his rival Mark Antony, deposed his lover Queen Cleopatra VII and annexed the Ptolemaic kingdom of Egypt to the Roman Empire. The province encompassed most of modern-day Egypt except for the Sinai Peninsula (which would later be conquered by Trajan). Aegyptus was bordered by the provinces of Creta et Cyrenaica to the West and Judaea to the East.
Fertile Crescent	The Fertile Crescent is a region in Western Asia. It includes the comparatively fertile regions of Mesopotamia and the Levant, delimited by the dry climate of the Syrian Desert to the south and the Anatolian highlands to the north. The region is often considered the cradle of civilization, saw the development of many of the earliest human civilizations, and is the birthplace of writing and the wheel.
Hama	Hama is a city on the banks of the Orontes River in central Syria north of Damascus. It is the provincial capital of the Hama Governorate. The city is the location of the historical city Hamath.
Lebanon	Lebanon is a mural size painting by Nabil Kanso depicting the Lebanese Civil War in a scene invoking the spirit and character of the people in the midst of horror and violence gripping the country. Amid the scene of chaos and devastation, two central figures reach across toward each other symbolically to represent the appeal for unity in defiance of the forces of division, destruction, and terror. Description Painted in oil on linen and completed in 1983, the painting Lebanon measures 28 feet (8.5 meters) long by 10 feet (3meters) tall.

Chapter 7. FROM SUEZ TO THE SIX-DAY WAR, 1957-1967

Palestine	Palestine (Greek: Παλαιστ?νη, Palaistine; Latin: Palaestina; Hebrew: ????????? Eretz-Yisra'el, (formerly also ????????, Palestina); Arabic: ??????? Filas?in, Falas?in, Filis?in) is a conventional name used, among others, to describe a geographic region between the Mediterranean Sea and the Jordan River, and various adjoining lands.

Other terms for the same area include Canaan, Zion, the Land of Israel, and the Holy Land. Southern Levant is another purely geographic term, often implemented for the region, which does not have political or theologic implications. |
| Republic | Republic is a Hungarian rock band formed in Budapest in 1989. Their style is a unique mix of Western rock music and traditional Hungarian folk music. The band is popular in its native country and among Hungarian speaking minorities elsewhere.

Members

The two founding members are László Bódi and Lászlo Attila Nagy. |
| State | The term state is used in various senses by Catholic theologians and spiritual writers.

It may be taken to signify a profession or calling in life, as where St. Paul says, in I Corinthians 7:20: "Let every man abide in the same calling in which he was called". States are classified in the Catholic Church as the clerical state, the religious state, and the secular state; and among religious states, again, we have those of the contemplative, the active, and the mixed orders. |
| Syria | Syria, officially the Syrian Arab Republic, is a country in Western Asia, bordering Lebanon and the Mediterranean Sea to the West, Turkey to the north, Iraq to the east, Jordan to the south, and Israel to the southwest. |

Chapter 7. FROM SUEZ TO THE SIX-DAY WAR, 1957-1967

The name Syria formerly comprised the entire region of the Levant, while the modern state encompasses the site of several ancient kingdoms and empires, including the Eblan civilization of the third millennium BC. In the Islamic era, its capital city, Damascus, was the seat of the Umayyad Empire and a provincial capital of the Mamluk Empire. Damascus is one of the oldest continuously inhabited cities in the world.

United Arab Republic	The United Arab Republic, was a union between Egypt and Syria. The union began in 1958 and existed until 1961 when Syria seceded from the union. Egypt continued to be known officially as the "United Arab Republic" until 1971. The President was Gamal Abdel Nasser.
Allies	Allies is a Christian rock band. They released six albums during the 1980s and early 1990s. Band members The most notable band members were guitarist Randy Thomas, formerly of the Jesus music group Sweet Comfort Band and vocalist Bob Carlisle.
Ancients	The Ancients were a group of English artists who were brought together by their attraction to archaism in art and admiration for the work of William Blake. The core members of the Ancients were Samuel Palmer, George Richmond, Edward Calvert. They met in Blake's apartment, dubbed the "House of Interpreter" and at the home of Samuel Palmer in the Kent village of Shoreham.
Politics	Aristotle's Politics is a work of political philosophy. The end of the Nicomachean Ethics declared that the inquiry into ethics necessarily follows into politics, and the two works are frequently considered to be parts of a larger treatise, or perhaps connected lectures, dealing with the "philosophy of human affairs." The title of the Politics literally means "the things concerning the polis." Composition

Chapter 7. FROM SUEZ TO THE SIX-DAY WAR, 1957-1967

The literary character of the Politics is subject to some dispute, growing out of the textual difficulties that attended the loss of Aristotle's works. Book III ends with a sentence that is repeated almost verbatim at the start of Book VII, while the intervening Books IV-VI seem to have a very different flavor from the rest; Book IV seems to refer several times back to the discussion of the best regime contained in Books VII-VIII. Some editors have therefore inserted Books VII-VIII after Book III. At the same time, however, references to the "discourses on politics" that occur in the Nicomachean Ethics suggest that the treatise as a whole ought to conclude with the discussion of education that occurs in Book VIII of the Politics, although it is not certain that Aristotle is referring to the Politics here.

Arabia

Arabia was a satrapy (province) of the Achaemenid Empire and later of the Sassanid Empire, by the name of Arabistan.

Achaemenid Era

Achaemenid Arabia corresponded to the lands between Egypt and Mesopotamia, known as Arabia Petraea. According to Herodotus, the Cambyses did not subdue the Arabs when he attacked Egypt in 525 BCE. His successor Darius the Great does not mention the Arabs in the Behistun inscription from the first years of his reign, but mentions them in later texts.

Baghdad

Baghdad is the capital of Iraq, as well as the coterminous Baghdad Governorate. With an estimated population between 7 and 7.5 million, it is the largest city in Iraq, the second largest city in the Arab World (after Cairo, Egypt), and the second largest city in Western Asia (after Tehran, Iran).

Located along the Tigris River, the city was founded in the 8th century and became the capital of the Abbasid Caliphate.

Husayn

Husayn is an Arabic name which is the diminutive of Hassan, meaning "good", "handsome" or "beautiful". It is commonly given as a male given name among Muslims, in honor of Husayn ibn Ali (626-680 AD). In some Persian sources the forms ?osayn, Hosayn, or Hossein is used.

187

Chapter 7. FROM SUEZ TO THE SIX-DAY WAR, 1957-1967

Iraq	Iraq ; officially the Republic of Iraq is a country in Western Asia spanning most of the northwestern end of the Zagros mountain range, the eastern part of the Syrian Desert and the northern part of the Arabian Desert.
	Iraq is bordered by Jordan to the west, Syria to the northwest, Turkey to the north, Iran to the east, and Kuwait and Saudi Arabia to the south. Iraq has a narrow section of coastline measuring 58 km (35 miles) on the northern Persian Gulf.
Saudi Arabia	The Kingdom of Saudi Arabia, commonly known as Saudi Arabia is, in land area, the third largest Arab country and the largest country in the Middle East. It is bordered by Jordan and Iraq on the north and northeast, Kuwait, Qatar and the United Arab Emirates on the east, Oman on the southeast, and Yemen on the south. It is also connected to Bahrain by the King Fahd Causeway.
Sharif	Sharif or Chérif is a traditional Arab tribal title given to those who serve as the protector of the tribe and all tribal assets, such as property, wells, and land. In origin, the word is an adjective meaning "noble", "highborn". The feminine singular is sharifa(h) (.
Catholic	The word catholic comes from the Greek phrase καθ?λου (kath'holou), meaning "on the whole," "according to the whole" or "in general", and is a combination of the Greek words κατ? meaning "about" and ?λος meaning "whole". The word in English can mean either "including a wide variety of things; all-embracing" or "of the Roman Catholic faith." as "relating to the historic doctrine and practice of the Western Church."
	It was first used to describe the Christian Church in the early 2nd century to emphasize its universal scope. In the context of Christian ecclesiology, it has a rich history and several usages.

189

Chapter 7. FROM SUEZ TO THE SIX-DAY WAR, 1957-1967

Druze	The Druze are an esoteric monotheistic religious community found primarily in Syria, Lebanon, Israel, and Jordan, which emerged during the 11th century from Ismailism and incorporated several elements of Gnosticism, Neoplatonism and other philosophies. Some Druze call themselves Ahl al-Tawhid "People of Unitarianism or Monotheism" or al-Muwa??idun "Unitarians, Monotheists."
	Location
	The Druze people reside primarily in Syria, Lebanon, and Israel. The Israeli Druze are mostly in Galilee (81%), around Haifa (19%), and in the Golan Heights.
Alliance	This article incorporates text from Easton's Bible Dictionary (1897), a publication now in the public domain.
	Abraham formed an alliance with some of the Canaanitish princes (Gen. 14:13), also with Abimelech (21:22-32). Joshua and the elders of Israel entered into an alliance with the Gibeonites (Josh. 9:3-27). When the Israelites entered Canaan they were forbidden to enter into alliances with the inhabitants of the country (Lev. 18:3, 4; 20:22, 23).
Mandate	In Christian theology, a mandate is an order given from God that must be obeyed without question. For example, the mandate given to Abraham to offer his son Isaac as a sacrifice to God. (Genesis 22:1)
Mandate	In Christian theology, a mandate is an order given from God that must be obeyed without question. For example, the mandate given to Abraham to offer his son Isaac as a sacrifice to God. (Genesis 22:1)
Ariel	Ariel is an Israeli settlement and a city in the central West Bank. Established in 1978, its population at the end of 2009 was 17,600, including 7,000 immigrants who came to Israel after 1990. It is the fourth largest Jewish settlement city in the West Bank., after Modi'in Illit, Beitar Illit, and Ma'ale Adumim.
	In Hebrew, Ariel, literally means 'Lion of God'.

Chapter 7. FROM SUEZ TO THE SIX-DAY WAR, 1957-1967

Beirut	35°30'47"E? / ?33.88694°N 35.51306°E
	Beirut is the capital and largest city of Lebanon with a population ranging from some 1 million to more than 2 million as of 2007. Located on a peninsula at the midpoint of Lebanon's coastline with the Mediterranean, it serves as the country's largest and main seaport, and also forms the Beirut Metropolitan Area, which consists of the city and its suburbs. The first mention of this metropolis is found in the ancient Egyptian Tell el Amarna letters, dating to the 15th century BC, and the city has been continuously inhabited since.
	Beirut holds Lebanon's seat of government, and plays a central role in the Lebanese economy with its city centre, Hamra, Verdun, and Ashrafieh-based corporate firms and banks.
Irgun	Irgun was a Zionist paramilitary group that operated in the British mandate of Palestine between 1931 and 1948. It was an offshoot of the earlier and larger Jewish paramilitary organization Haganah . Since the group originally broke from the Haganah it became known as the Haganah Bet, or alternatively as Haganah Ha'leumit (????? ???????) or Ha'ma'amad (??????). Irgun members were absorbed into the Israel Defence Forces at the start of the 1948 Arab-Israeli war.
Lebanese Civil War	The Lebanese Civil War was a multifaceted civil war in Lebanon. The war lasted from 1975 to 1990 and resulted in an estimated 130,000 to 250,000 civilian fatalities. Another one million people (a quarter of the population) were wounded, and today approximately 350,000 people remain displaced, the majority of them Christian Lebanese who were forced out of the Chouf mountains.
Arab world	The Arab world refers to Arabic-speaking countries stretching from the Atlantic Ocean in the west to the Arabian Sea in the east, and from the Mediterranean Sea in the north to the Horn of Africa and the Indian Ocean in the southeast.
	It consists of 22 countries and territories with a combined population of 360 million people straddling North Africa and Western Asia.

Chapter 7. FROM SUEZ TO THE SIX-DAY WAR, 1957-1967

The sentiment of Arab nationalism arose in the second half of the 19th century along with other nationalisms within the failing Ottoman Empire.

World

WORLD Magazine is a biweekly Christian news magazine, published in the United States of America by God's World Publications, a non-profit 501(c)(3) organization based in Asheville, North Carolina. WORLD differs from most other news magazines in that its declared perspective is one of conservative evangelical Protestantism. Its mission statement is "To report, interpret, and illustrate the news in a timely, accurate, enjoyable, and arresting fashion from a perspective committed to the Bible as the inerrant Word of God."

Each issue features both U.S. and international news, cultural analysis, editorials and commentary, as well as book, music and movie reviews.

Aswan

Aswan, formerly spelled Assuan, is a city in the south of Egypt, the capital of the Aswan Governorate.

It stands on the east bank of the Nile at the first cataract and is a busy market and tourist centre. The modern city has expanded and includes the formerly separate community on the island of Elephantine.

Aswan Dam

The Aswan Dam is an embankment dam situated across the Nile River in Aswan, Egypt. Since the 1950s, the name commonly refers to the High Dam, which is larger and newer than the Aswan Low Dam, which was first completed in 1902. Following Egypt's independence from the United Kingdom, the High Dam was constructed between 1960 and 1970. It aimed to increase economic production by further regulating the annual river flooding and providing storage of water for agriculture, and later, to generate hydroelectricity. The dam has had a significant impact on the economy and culture of Egypt.

Suez Crisis

The Suez Crisis, also referred to as the Tripartite Aggression, was a war fought by Britain, France, and Israel against Egypt beginning on 29 October 1956.

Chapter 7. FROM SUEZ TO THE SIX-DAY WAR, 1957-1967

The attack followed Egypt's decision of 26 July 1956 to nationalize the Suez Canal, after the withdrawal of an offer by Britain and the United States to fund the building of the Aswan Dam, which was partly in response to Egypt recognizing the People's Republic of China during the height of tensions between China and Taiwan. Britain and France were also strongly opposed to Nasser's plan to annex the Sudan.

Arafat

Arafat is a surname or given name, and may refer to:

- Yasser Arafat
- Fathi Arafat Palestinian physician
- Moussa Arafat cousin of Yasser Arafat
- Raed Arafat Romanian physician
- Suha Arafat widow of Yasser Arafat
- Yasir Arafat , Pakistani cricketer

Abbas

Abbas means "lion" in Arabic. (Austere: (1) severely simple in appearance. (2) strict, stern).

Emir

Emir, ("commander" or "general", also "prince" ; also transliterated as amir, aamir or ameer) is a high title of nobility or office, used throughout the Muslim world. Emirs are usually considered high-ranking sheikhs, but in monarchical states the term is also used for princes, with "Emirate" being analogous to principality in this sense.

While emir is the predominant spelling in English and many other languages, amir, closer to the original Arabic, is more common for its numerous compounds (e.g. admiral) and in individual names.

Jerusalem

Jerusalem [ii] is the capital of Israel, though not internationally recognized as such.[iii] If the area and population of East Jerusalem is included, it is Israel's largest city in both population and area, with a population of 763,800 residents over an area of 125.1 km^2 (48.3 sq mi).[iv] Located in the Judean Mountains, between the Mediterranean Sea and the northern edge of the Dead Sea, modern Jerusalem has grown far beyond the boundaries of the Old City.

Chapter 7. FROM SUEZ TO THE SIX-DAY WAR, 1957-1967

Jerusalem is a holy city to the three major Abrahamic religions--Judaism, Christianity and Islam. In Judaism, Jerusalem has been the holiest city since, according to the Torah, King David of Israel first established it as the capital of the united Kingdom of Israel in c. 1000 BCE, and his son Solomon commissioned the building of the First Temple in the city.

Temple

In the Latter Day Saint movement, a temple is a building dedicated to be a house of God and is reserved for special forms of worship. A temple differs from a church meetinghouse, which is used for weekly worship services. Temples have been a significant part of the Latter Day Saint movement since early in its inception.

Temple Mount

The Temple Mount, also known in the Bible as Mount Moriah (some also identify it with the biblical Mount Zion) and by Muslims as the Noble Sanctuary (Bait-ul-Muqaddas), is a religious site in the Old City of Jerusalem.

Judaism regards the Temple Mount as the place where God chose the Divine Presence to rest (Isa 8:18); it was from here the world expanded into its present form and where God gathered the dust used to create the first man, Adam.{According to the sages of the Talmud[13]} The site is the location of Abraham's binding of Isaac, and of two Jewish Temples. According to the Bible the site should function as the center of all national life - government, judicial and, of course, religious center (Deut 12:5-26; 14:23-25; 15:20; 16:2-16; 17:8-10; 26: 2; 31: 11; Isa 2: 2-5; Oba 1:21; Psa 48) .

Ahmad

Ahmad and Ahmed are the principal transliterations of the Arabic given name . The latter name comes from the Arabic triconsonantal root of ?-M-D, meaning "highly praised", implying "one who constantly thanks Allah".

Etymology

One of the Islamic prophet Muhammad's many names is Ahmad, the name "Muhammad" pre-dating "Ahmad".

Kuwait	The State of Kuwait is a sovereign Arab nation situated in the northeast of the Arabian Peninsula in Western Asia. It is bordered by Saudi Arabia to the south, and Iraq to the north. It lies on the northwestern shore of the Persian Gulf.
Prime	Prime, is a fixed time of prayer of the traditional Divine Office (Canonical Hours), said at the first hour of daylight (approximately 6:00 a.m)., between the morning Hour of Lauds and the 9 a.m. Hour of Terce. It is part of the Christian liturgies of Eastern Christianity, but in the Latin Rite it was suppressed by the Second Vatican Council. However, clergy who have an obligation to celebrate the Liturgy of the Hours may still fulfil their obligation by using the Roman Breviary promulgated by Pope John XXIII in 1962, which contains the Hour of Prime.
Allon Plan	The Allon Plan was an Israeli proposal of the late 1960s to partition the West Bank, captured from Jordan in the Six-Day War of June 1967, between Israel and Jordan. It is named after Yigal Allon, who drafted it shortly after the war. The broad aim of the plan was to annex most of the Jordan Valley from the river to the eastern slopes of the West Bank hill ridge, East Jerusalem, and the Etzion bloc to Israel.
West Bank	The West Bank of the Jordan River is the landlocked geographical eastern part of the Palestinian territories located in the Western Asia. To the west, north, and south, the West Bank shares borders with the state of Israel. To the east, across the Jordan River, lies the Hashemite Kingdom of Jordan.
Israeli settlement	An Israeli settlement is an Israeli civilian community on land that was captured by Israel during the Six-Day War and is considered by the international community (excluding Israel) to be occupied territory. Such settlements currently exist in the West Bank, East Jerusalem, and the Golan Heights. The International Court of Justice and the international community say these settlements are illegal,.
Nuri	Nuri is a place in modern Sudan on the south (east) side of the Nile. Close to it, there are pyramids belonging to Nubian kings. Nuri is situated about 15 km north of Sanam, and 10 km from Jebel Barkal.

Chapter 7. FROM SUEZ TO THE SIX-DAY WAR, 1957-1967

Arab	The proper name Arab or "Arabian" (and cognates in other languages) has been used to translate several different but similar sounding words in ancient and classical texts which do not necessarily have the same meaning or origin. Grunebaum, in his book Classical Islam said that an approximate translation is "passerby" or "nomad". Will Durant, in The Age of Faith, said that Arab meant Arid.
Zionism	Zionism is a Jewish political movement that, in its broadest sense, has supported the self-determination of the Jewish people in a sovereign Jewish national homeland. Since the establishment of the State of Israel, the Zionist movement continues primarily to advocate on behalf of the Jewish state and address threats to its continued existence and security. In a less common usage, the term may also refer to 1) non-political, Cultural Zionism, founded and represented most prominently by Ahad Ha'am; and 2) political support for the State of Israel by non-Jews, as in Christian Zionism.
Response	A response is the second half of one of a set of preces, the said or sung answer by the congregation or choir to a versicle said or sung by an officiant or cantor. In the following opening of the Anglican service of Evening Prayer according to the Book of Common Prayer (BCP), the first line is the versicle and the second is the response. In some liturgical books (such as hymnals or breviaries) the symbol "R/" or "?" is used to denote a response.
Peace	Peace is an Athenian Old Comedy written and produced by the Greek playwright Aristophanes. It won second prize at the City Dionysia where it was staged just a few days before the ratification of the Peace of Nicias (421 BC), which promised to end the ten year old Peloponnesian War. The play is notable for its joyous anticipation of peace and for its celebration of a return to an idyllic life in the countryside.

Chapter 8. WAR AND THE SEARCH FOR PEACE IN THE MIDDLE EAST, 1967-1976

Cold War	Cold War is a video game developed by Czech developer Mindware Studios and published by DreamCatcher Games (Linux Game Publishing for Linux). The game is similar to the Splinter Cell series of games in that it uses a stealth-action system of gameplay. The game distinguishes itself by adding an invention system where the player can use seemingly useless objects to create tools and weapons.
East Jerusalem	East Jerusalem refers to the parts of Jerusalem captured by Jordan in the 1948 Arab-Israeli War and then taken by Israel in the 1967 Six-Day War. It includes Jerusalem's Old City and some of the holiest sites of Judaism, Christianity, and Islam, such as the Temple Mount, Western Wall, Al-Aqsa Mosque, and the Church of the Holy Sepulchre. The term "East Jerusalem" may refer to either the area under Jordanian rule between 1949 and 1967 which was incorporated into the municipality of Jerusalem after 1967, covering some 70 km^2 (27 sq mi), or the territory of the pre-1967 Jordanian municipality, covering 6.4 km^2 (2.5 sq mi).
Jerusalem	Jerusalem [ii] is the capital of Israel, though not internationally recognized as such.[iii] If the area and population of East Jerusalem is included, it is Israel's largest city in both population and area, with a population of 763,800 residents over an area of 125.1 km^2 (48.3 sq mi).[iv] Located in the Judean Mountains, between the Mediterranean Sea and the northern edge of the Dead Sea, modern Jerusalem has grown far beyond the boundaries of the Old City. Jerusalem is a holy city to the three major Abrahamic religions--Judaism, Christianity and Islam. In Judaism, Jerusalem has been the holiest city since, according to the Torah, King David of Israel first established it as the capital of the united Kingdom of Israel in c. 1000 BCE, and his son Solomon commissioned the building of the First Temple in the city.
Palestine	Palestine (Greek: Παλαιστ?νη, Palaistine; Latin: Palaestina; Hebrew: ????????? Eretz-Yisra'el, (formerly also ????????, Palestina); Arabic: ??????? Filas?in, Falas?in, Filis?in) is a conventional name used, among others, to describe a geographic region between the Mediterranean Sea and the Jordan River, and various adjoining lands. Other terms for the same area include Canaan, Zion, the Land of Israel, and the Holy Land. Southern Levant is another purely geographic term, often implemented for the region, which does not have political or theologic implications.

Chapter 8. WAR AND THE SEARCH FOR PEACE IN THE MIDDLE EAST, 1967-1976

Zionism	Zionism is a Jewish political movement that, in its broadest sense, has supported the self-determination of the Jewish people in a sovereign Jewish national homeland. Since the establishment of the State of Israel, the Zionist movement continues primarily to advocate on behalf of the Jewish state and address threats to its continued existence and security. In a less common usage, the term may also refer to 1) non-political, Cultural Zionism, founded and represented most prominently by Ahad Ha'am; and 2) political support for the State of Israel by non-Jews, as in Christian Zionism.
Response	A response is the second half of one of a set of preces, the said or sung answer by the congregation or choir to a versicle said or sung by an officiant or cantor. In the following opening of the Anglican service of Evening Prayer according to the Book of Common Prayer (BCP), the first line is the versicle and the second is the response. In some liturgical books (such as hymnals or breviaries) the symbol "R/" or "?" is used to denote a response.
Israeli settlement	An Israeli settlement is an Israeli civilian community on land that was captured by Israel during the Six-Day War and is considered by the international community (excluding Israel) to be occupied territory. Such settlements currently exist in the West Bank, East Jerusalem, and the Golan Heights. The International Court of Justice and the international community say these settlements are illegal,.
Syria	Syria, officially the Syrian Arab Republic, is a country in Western Asia, bordering Lebanon and the Mediterranean Sea to the West, Turkey to the north, Iraq to the east, Jordan to the south, and Israel to the southwest.

The name Syria formerly comprised the entire region of the Levant, while the modern state encompasses the site of several ancient kingdoms and empires, including the Eblan civilization of the third millennium BC. In the Islamic era, its capital city, Damascus, was the seat of the Umayyad Empire and a provincial capital of the Mamluk Empire. Damascus is one of the oldest continuously inhabited cities in the world.

West Bank

The West Bank of the Jordan River is the landlocked geographical eastern part of the Palestinian territories located in the Western Asia. To the west, north, and south, the West Bank shares borders with the state of Israel. To the east, across the Jordan River, lies the Hashemite Kingdom of Jordan.

Allon Plan

The Allon Plan was an Israeli proposal of the late 1960s to partition the West Bank, captured from Jordan in the Six-Day War of June 1967, between Israel and Jordan. It is named after Yigal Allon, who drafted it shortly after the war.

The broad aim of the plan was to annex most of the Jordan Valley from the river to the eastern slopes of the West Bank hill ridge, East Jerusalem, and the Etzion bloc to Israel.

Arabia

Arabia was a satrapy (province) of the Achaemenid Empire and later of the Sassanid Empire, by the name of Arabistan.

Achaemenid Era

Achaemenid Arabia corresponded to the lands between Egypt and Mesopotamia, known as Arabia Petraea. According to Herodotus, the Cambyses did not subdue the Arabs when he attacked Egypt in 525 BCE. His successor Darius the Great does not mention the Arabs in the Behistun inscription from the first years of his reign, but mentions them in later texts.

Chapter 8. WAR AND THE SEARCH FOR PEACE IN THE MIDDLE EAST, 1967-1976

Arafat	Arafat is a surname or given name, and may refer to: • Yasser Arafat • Fathi Arafat Palestinian physician • Moussa Arafat cousin of Yasser Arafat • Raed Arafat Romanian physician • Suha Arafat widow of Yasser Arafat • Yasir Arafat , Pakistani cricketer .
Egypt	The Roman province of Egypt was established in 30 BC after Octavian (the future emperor Augustus) defeated his rival Mark Antony, deposed his lover Queen Cleopatra VII and annexed the Ptolemaic kingdom of Egypt to the Roman Empire. The province encompassed most of modern-day Egypt except for the Sinai Peninsula (which would later be conquered by Trajan). Aegyptus was bordered by the provinces of Creta et Cyrenaica to the West and Judaea to the East.
Republic	Republic is a Hungarian rock band formed in Budapest in 1989. Their style is a unique mix of Western rock music and traditional Hungarian folk music. The band is popular in its native country and among Hungarian speaking minorities elsewhere. Members The two founding members are László Bódi and Lászlo Attila Nagy.
Saudi Arabia	The Kingdom of Saudi Arabia, commonly known as Saudi Arabia is, in land area, the third largest Arab country and the largest country in the Middle East. It is bordered by Jordan and Iraq on the north and northeast, Kuwait, Qatar and the United Arab Emirates on the east, Oman on the southeast, and Yemen on the south. It is also connected to Bahrain by the King Fahd Causeway.
Sharif	Sharif or Chérif is a traditional Arab tribal title given to those who serve as the protector of the tribe and all tribal assets, such as property, wells, and land. In origin, the word is an adjective meaning "noble", "highborn". The feminine singular is sharifa(h) (.

211

Chapter 8. WAR AND THE SEARCH FOR PEACE IN THE MIDDLE EAST, 1967-1976

State	The term state is used in various senses by Catholic theologians and spiritual writers.
	It may be taken to signify a profession or calling in life, as where St. Paul says, in I Corinthians 7:20: "Let every man abide in the same calling in which he was called". States are classified in the Catholic Church as the clerical state, the religious state, and the secular state; and among religious states, again, we have those of the contemplative, the active, and the mixed orders.
Politics	Aristotle's Politics is a work of political philosophy. The end of the Nicomachean Ethics declared that the inquiry into ethics necessarily follows into politics, and the two works are frequently considered to be parts of a larger treatise, or perhaps connected lectures, dealing with the "philosophy of human affairs." The title of the Politics literally means "the things concerning the polis."
	Composition
	The literary character of the Politics is subject to some dispute, growing out of the textual difficulties that attended the loss of Aristotle's works. Book III ends with a sentence that is repeated almost verbatim at the start of Book VII, while the intervening Books IV-VI seem to have a very different flavor from the rest; Book IV seems to refer several times back to the discussion of the best regime contained in Books VII-VIII. Some editors have therefore inserted Books VII-VIII after Book III. At the same time, however, references to the "discourses on politics" that occur in the Nicomachean Ethics suggest that the treatise as a whole ought to conclude with the discussion of education that occurs in Book VIII of the Politics, although it is not certain that Aristotle is referring to the Politics here.
Arab	The proper name Arab or "Arabian" (and cognates in other languages) has been used to translate several different but similar sounding words in ancient and classical texts which do not necessarily have the same meaning or origin. Grunebaum, in his book Classical Islam said that an approximate translation is "passerby" or "nomad". Will Durant, in The Age of Faith, said that Arab meant Arid.

Chapter 8. WAR AND THE SEARCH FOR PEACE IN THE MIDDLE EAST, 1967-1976

Ancients	The Ancients were a group of English artists who were brought together by their attraction to archaism in art and admiration for the work of William Blake. The core members of the Ancients were Samuel Palmer, George Richmond, Edward Calvert. They met in Blake's apartment, dubbed the "House of Interpreter" and at the home of Samuel Palmer in the Kent village of Shoreham.
Abbas	Abbas means "lion" in Arabic. (Austere: (1) severely simple in appearance. (2) strict, stern).
Prime	Prime, is a fixed time of prayer of the traditional Divine Office (Canonical Hours), said at the first hour of daylight (approximately 6:00 a.m)., between the morning Hour of Lauds and the 9 a.m. Hour of Terce. It is part of the Christian liturgies of Eastern Christianity, but in the Latin Rite it was suppressed by the Second Vatican Council. However, clergy who have an obligation to celebrate the Liturgy of the Hours may still fulfil their obligation by using the Roman Breviary promulgated by Pope John XXIII in 1962, which contains the Hour of Prime.
Emir	Emir, ("commander" or "general", also "prince" ; also transliterated as amir, aamir or ameer) is a high title of nobility or office, used throughout the Muslim world. Emirs are usually considered high-ranking sheikhs, but in monarchical states the term is also used for princes, with "Emirate" being analogous to principality in this sense. While emir is the predominant spelling in English and many other languages, amir, closer to the original Arabic, is more common for its numerous compounds (e.g. admiral) and in individual names.
Husayn	Husayn is an Arabic name which is the diminutive of Hassan, meaning "good", "handsome" or "beautiful". It is commonly given as a male given name among Muslims, in honor of Husayn ibn Ali (626-680 AD). In some Persian sources the forms ?osayn, Hosayn, or Hossein is used.
Ahmad	Ahmad and Ahmed are the principal transliterations of the Arabic given name . The latter name comes from the Arabic triconsonantal root of ?-M-D, meaning "highly praised", implying "one who constantly thanks Allah". Etymology

Chapter 8. WAR AND THE SEARCH FOR PEACE IN THE MIDDLE EAST, 1967-1976

One of the Islamic prophet Muhammad's many names is Ahmad, the name "Muhammad" pre-dating "Ahmad".

Arab nationalism	Arab nationalism is a nationalist ideology celebrating the glories of Arab civilization, the language and literature of the Arabs, calling for rejuvenation and political union in the Arab world. Its central premise is that the peoples of the Arab World, from the Atlantic Ocean to the Arabian Sea, constitute one nation bound together by common linguistic, cultural, religious, and historical heritage, One of the primary goals of Arab nationalism is the end of Western influence in the Arab World, seen as a "nemesis" of Arab strength, and the removal of those Arab governments considered to be dependent upon Western power. It rose to prominence with the weakening and defeat of the Ottoman Empire in the early 20th century and declined after the defeat of the Arab armies in the Six Day War.
Damascus	Damascus is the capital and the second largest city of Syria as well as one of the country's 14 governorates. The Damascus Governorate is ruled by a governor appointed by the Minister of Interior. In addition to being the oldest continuously inhabited city in the world, Damascus is a major cultural and religious center of the Levant.
Front	Front was first published by Cabal Communications in 1998, it was created to rival IPC's publication Loaded, catering to a demographic of 16-25 year-old males. It began as part of the British "lads' mag" genre of magazines though the covers rejects this description with the statement "Front is no lads' mag".
	Whilst a major selling point is the photo-shoots of models, the magazine also focuses heavily on music, films, gadgets and games, plus sections on fashion and sport.
Lebanon	Lebanon is a mural size painting by Nabil Kanso depicting the Lebanese Civil War in a scene invoking the spirit and character of the people in the midst of horror and violence gripping the country. Amid the scene of chaos and devastation, two central figures reach across toward each other symbolically to represent the appeal for unity in defiance of the forces of division, destruction, and terror.
	Description

	Painted in oil on linen and completed in 1983, the painting Lebanon measures 28 feet (8.5 meters) long by 10 feet (3meters) tall.
Mandate	In Christian theology, a mandate is an order given from God that must be obeyed without question. For example, the mandate given to Abraham to offer his son Isaac as a sacrifice to God. (Genesis 22:1)
Mandate Palestine	Mandate Palestine existed while the British Mandate for Palestine, which formally began in September 1923 and terminated in May 1948, was in effect. It consisted of the part of the Mandate territory to the west of a line which, in the north, followed the Jordan River. In 1917, during the First World War, Britain defeated the Ottoman Turkish forces and occupied and set up a military administration in Palestine and Syria.
Catholic	The word catholic comes from the Greek phrase καθ?λου (kath'holou), meaning "on the whole," "according to the whole" or "in general", and is a combination of the Greek words κατ? meaning "about" and ?λος meaning "whole". The word in English can mean either "including a wide variety of things; all-embracing" or "of the Roman Catholic faith." as "relating to the historic doctrine and practice of the Western Church." It was first used to describe the Christian Church in the early 2nd century to emphasize its universal scope. In the context of Christian ecclesiology, it has a rich history and several usages.
Druze	The Druze are an esoteric monotheistic religious community found primarily in Syria, Lebanon, Israel, and Jordan, which emerged during the 11th century from Ismailism and incorporated several elements of Gnosticism, Neoplatonism and other philosophies. Some Druze call themselves Ahl al-Tawhid "People of Unitarianism or Monotheism" or al-Muwa??idun "Unitarians, Monotheists." Location

	The Druze people reside primarily in Syria, Lebanon, and Israel. The Israeli Druze are mostly in Galilee (81%), around Haifa (19%), and in the Golan Heights.
Suez Crisis	The Suez Crisis, also referred to as the Tripartite Aggression, was a war fought by Britain, France, and Israel against Egypt beginning on 29 October 1956.
	The attack followed Egypt's decision of 26 July 1956 to nationalize the Suez Canal, after the withdrawal of an offer by Britain and the United States to fund the building of the Aswan Dam, which was partly in response to Egypt recognizing the People's Republic of China during the height of tensions between China and Taiwan. Britain and France were also strongly opposed to Nasser's plan to annex the Sudan.
Joseph	The Bible: Joseph is a German/Italian/American television movie from 1995, which tells the story of Joseph from the Old Testament.
	Plot
	The opening scene is at the slave market of Avaris. Potiphar, the chief steward of the Pharaoh, is looking to buy a slave.
Hebron	Hebron, is located in the southern West Bank, 30 km (19 mi) south of Jerusalem. Nestled in the Judean Mountains, it lies 930 meters (3,050 ft) above sea level. It is the largest city in the West Bank and home to around 165,000 Palestinians, and over 500 Jewish settlers concentrated in and around the old quarter.
Difference	Difference is a key concept of continental philosophy, opposed to Identity.

221

Gilles Deleuze's Difference and Repetition (1968) was an attempt, to think Difference as having an ontological privilege over Identity, inversing the traditional relationship between those two concepts.

Peace	Peace is an Athenian Old Comedy written and produced by the Greek playwright Aristophanes. It won second prize at the City Dionysia where it was staged just a few days before the ratification of the Peace of Nicias (421 BC), which promised to end the ten year old Peloponnesian War. The play is notable for its joyous anticipation of peace and for its celebration of a return to an idyllic life in the countryside.
Emunim	Emunim is a moshav in central Israel. Located near Ashdod, it falls under the jurisdiction of Be'er Tuvia Regional Council. In 2006 it had a population of 732
	The moshav was founded in 1950 by immigrants from Egypt, on the land of the Palestinian village of Beit Daras.
Henry	Henry is an English male given name and a surname, from the Old French Henry derived itself from the Germanic name Haimric, which was derived from the word elements haim, meaning "home" and ric, meaning "power, ruler". Harry, its English short form, was considered the "spoken form" of Henry in medieval England. Most English kings named Henry were called Harry.
Iraq	Iraq ; officially the Republic of Iraq is a country in Western Asia spanning most of the northwestern end of the Zagros mountain range, the eastern part of the Syrian Desert and the northern part of the Arabian Desert.
	Iraq is bordered by Jordan to the west, Syria to the northwest, Turkey to the north, Iran to the east, and Kuwait and Saudi Arabia to the south. Iraq has a narrow section of coastline measuring 58 km (35 miles) on the northern Persian Gulf.

Chapter 8. WAR AND THE SEARCH FOR PEACE IN THE MIDDLE EAST, 1967-1976

Kuwait	The State of Kuwait is a sovereign Arab nation situated in the northeast of the Arabian Peninsula in Western Asia. It is bordered by Saudi Arabia to the south, and Iraq to the north. It lies on the northwestern shore of the Persian Gulf.
Judea	35°18′23″E? / ?31.69889°N 35.30639°E Judea, when Roman Judea was renamed Syria Palaestina following the Jewish Bar Kokhba revolt. Etymology The name Judea is a Greek and Roman adaptation of the name "Judah", which originally encompassed the territory of the Israelite tribe of that name and later of the ancient Kingdom of Judah. It was the name in use in English throughout history until the Jordanian occupation of the area.
Samaria	Samaria is a term used for a mountainous region roughly corresponding to the northern part of the West Bank. According to 1 Kings 16:24, it is derived from the individual [or clan] Shemer, from whom Omri purchased the site. The name was the only name used for this area from ancient times until the Jordanian conquest of 1948, at which point the Jordanian occupiers coined the term West Bank.
Aqaba	Aqaba is a coastal town in the far south of Jordan. It is the capital of Aqaba Governorate. Aqaba is strategically important to Jordan as it is the country's only seaport.
Sharm el-Sheikh	Sharm el-Sheikh is a city situated on the southern tip of the Sinai Peninsula, in South Sinai Governorate, Egypt, on the coastal strip along the Red Sea with a population of approximately 35,000 (2008). Sharm el-Sheikh is the administrative hub of Egypt's South Sinai Governorate which includes the smaller coastal towns of Dahab and Nuweiba as well as the mountainous interior, Saint Catherine's Monastery and Mount Sinai. Name

Chapter 8. WAR AND THE SEARCH FOR PEACE IN THE MIDDLE EAST, 1967-1976

Sharm el-Sheikh is sometimes called the "City of Peace", referring to the large number of international peace conferences that have been held there.

Ariel

Ariel is an Israeli settlement and a city in the central West Bank. Established in 1978, its population at the end of 2009 was 17,600, including 7,000 immigrants who came to Israel after 1990. It is the fourth largest Jewish settlement city in the West Bank., after Modi'in Illit, Beitar Illit, and Ma'ale Adumim.

In Hebrew, Ariel, literally means 'Lion of God'.

Libya

Libya was a satrapy of the Achaemenid Empire according to King Darius I of Persia Naqshe Rustam and King Xerxes I of Persia' Daiva inscription. It is also mentioned as being part of the 6th district by Herodotus, which also included Cyrene, a Greek colony in Libya. When King Cambyses II of Persia conquered Egypt, the king of Cyrene, Arcesilaus III, sided with Persia.

227

Orthodox	Orthodox Basketball Club formerly known as Fastlink Basketball Club is a Jordanian basketball club based in Amman, Jordan. They compete in the Jordanian Basketball Federation.

Tournament records

WABA Champions Cup

- 1999: Champions
- 2001: 2nd place
- 2002: 2nd place
- 2004: 1st place
- 2008: 2nd place
- 2009: 1st place

Asia Champions Cup

- 1988: 5th place
- 1996: 7th place
- 1999: 6th place

. |
| Correspondence | In theology, correspondence is the relationship between spiritual and natural realities, or between mental and physical realities. The term was coined by the 18th century theologian Emanuel Swedenborg in his Arcana Coelestia (1749-1756) and Heaven and Hell (1758) and other works.

Swedenborg states that there is a correspondence between, for example: thought and speech, between intention and action, between mind and body, and between God and creation. |

229

Chapter 9. LEBANON, THE WEST BANK, AND THE CAMP DAVID ACCORDS

Camp David Accords	The Camp David Accords were signed by Egyptian President Anwar El Sadat and Israeli Prime Minister Menachem Begin on September 17, 1978, following thirteen days of secret negotiations at Camp David. The two framework agreements were signed at the White House, and were witnessed by United States President Jimmy Carter. The second of these frameworks, A Framework for the Conclusion of a Peace Treaty between Egypt and Israel, led directly to the 1979 Egypt-Israel Peace Treaty, and resulted in Sadat and Begin sharing the 1978 Nobel Peace Prize.
Egypt	The Roman province of Egypt was established in 30 BC after Octavian (the future emperor Augustus) defeated his rival Mark Antony, deposed his lover Queen Cleopatra VII and annexed the Ptolemaic kingdom of Egypt to the Roman Empire. The province encompassed most of modern-day Egypt except for the Sinai Peninsula (which would later be conquered by Trajan). Aegyptus was bordered by the provinces of Creta et Cyrenaica to the West and Judaea to the East.
Israeli settlement	An Israeli settlement is an Israeli civilian community on land that was captured by Israel during the Six-Day War and is considered by the international community (excluding Israel) to be occupied territory. Such settlements currently exist in the West Bank, East Jerusalem, and the Golan Heights. The International Court of Justice and the international community say these settlements are illegal,.
Peace	Peace is an Athenian Old Comedy written and produced by the Greek playwright Aristophanes. It won second prize at the City Dionysia where it was staged just a few days before the ratification of the Peace of Nicias (421 BC), which promised to end the ten year old Peloponnesian War. The play is notable for its joyous anticipation of peace and for its celebration of a return to an idyllic life in the countryside.
State	The term state is used in various senses by Catholic theologians and spiritual writers.

It may be taken to signify a profession or calling in life, as where St. Paul says, in I Corinthians 7:20: "Let every man abide in the same calling in which he was called". States are classified in the Catholic Church as the clerical state, the religious state, and the secular state; and among religious states, again, we have those of the contemplative, the active, and the mixed orders.

| Difference | Difference is a key concept of continental philosophy, opposed to Identity. |
| | |

Gilles Deleuze's Difference and Repetition (1968) was an attempt, to think Difference as having an ontological privilege over Identity, inversing the traditional relationship between those two concepts.

| Prime | Prime, is a fixed time of prayer of the traditional Divine Office (Canonical Hours), said at the first hour of daylight (approximately 6:00 a.m)., between the morning Hour of Lauds and the 9 a.m. Hour of Terce. It is part of the Christian liturgies of Eastern Christianity, but in the Latin Rite it was suppressed by the Second Vatican Council. However, clergy who have an obligation to celebrate the Liturgy of the Hours may still fulfil their obligation by using the Roman Breviary promulgated by Pope John XXIII in 1962, which contains the Hour of Prime. |

| Catholic | The word catholic comes from the Greek phrase καθ?λου (kath'holou), meaning "on the whole," "according to the whole" or "in general", and is a combination of the Greek words κατ? meaning "about" and ?λος meaning "whole". The word in English can mean either "including a wide variety of things; all-embracing" or "of the Roman Catholic faith." as "relating to the historic doctrine and practice of the Western Church." |

It was first used to describe the Christian Church in the early 2nd century to emphasize its universal scope. In the context of Christian ecclesiology, it has a rich history and several usages.

233

CRAM101

Chapter 9. LEBANON, THE WEST BANK, AND THE CAMP DAVID ACCORDS

Druze	The Druze are an esoteric monotheistic religious community found primarily in Syria, Lebanon, Israel, and Jordan, which emerged during the 11th century from Ismailism and incorporated several elements of Gnosticism, Neoplatonism and other philosophies. Some Druze call themselves Ahl al-Tawhid "People of Unitarianism or Monotheism" or al-Muwa??idun "Unitarians, Monotheists."
	Location
	The Druze people reside primarily in Syria, Lebanon, and Israel. The Israeli Druze are mostly in Galilee (81%), around Haifa (19%), and in the Golan Heights.
Lebanon	Lebanon is a mural size painting by Nabil Kanso depicting the Lebanese Civil War in a scene invoking the spirit and character of the people in the midst of horror and violence gripping the country. Amid the scene of chaos and devastation, two central figures reach across toward each other symbolically to represent the appeal for unity in defiance of the forces of division, destruction, and terror.
	Description
	Painted in oil on linen and completed in 1983, the painting Lebanon measures 28 feet (8.5 meters) long by 10 feet (3meters) tall.
Politics	Aristotle's Politics is a work of political philosophy. The end of the Nicomachean Ethics declared that the inquiry into ethics necessarily follows into politics, and the two works are frequently considered to be parts of a larger treatise, or perhaps connected lectures, dealing with the "philosophy of human affairs." The title of the Politics literally means "the things concerning the polis."
	Composition

235

The literary character of the Politics is subject to some dispute, growing out of the textual difficulties that attended the loss of Aristotle's works. Book III ends with a sentence that is repeated almost verbatim at the start of Book VII, while the intervening Books IV-VI seem to have a very different flavor from the rest; Book IV seems to refer several times back to the discussion of the best regime contained in Books VII-VIII. Some editors have therefore inserted Books VII-VIII after Book III. At the same time, however, references to the "discourses on politics" that occur in the Nicomachean Ethics suggest that the treatise as a whole ought to conclude with the discussion of education that occurs in Book VIII of the Politics, although it is not certain that Aristotle is referring to the Politics here.

| Arab nationalism | Arab nationalism is a nationalist ideology celebrating the glories of Arab civilization, the language and literature of the Arabs, calling for rejuvenation and political union in the Arab world. Its central premise is that the peoples of the Arab World, from the Atlantic Ocean to the Arabian Sea, constitute one nation bound together by common linguistic, cultural, religious, and historical heritage, One of the primary goals of Arab nationalism is the end of Western influence in the Arab World, seen as a "nemesis" of Arab strength, and the removal of those Arab governments considered to be dependent upon Western power. It rose to prominence with the weakening and defeat of the Ottoman Empire in the early 20th century and declined after the defeat of the Arab armies in the Six Day War. |

| Front | Front was first published by Cabal Communications in 1998, it was created to rival IPC's publication Loaded, catering to a demographic of 16-25 year-old males. It began as part of the British "lads' mag" genre of magazines though the covers rejects this description with the statement "Front is no lads' mag".

Whilst a major selling point is the photo-shoots of models, the magazine also focuses heavily on music, films, gadgets and games, plus sections on fashion and sport. |

| Hebron | Hebron, is located in the southern West Bank, 30 km (19 mi) south of Jerusalem. Nestled in the Judean Mountains, it lies 930 meters (3,050 ft) above sea level. It is the largest city in the West Bank and home to around 165,000 Palestinians, and over 500 Jewish settlers concentrated in and around the old quarter. |

237

Cram101

Chapter 9. LEBANON, THE WEST BANK, AND THE CAMP DAVID ACCORDS

Lebanese Civil War	The Lebanese Civil War was a multifaceted civil war in Lebanon. The war lasted from 1975 to 1990 and resulted in an estimated 130,000 to 250,000 civilian fatalities. Another one million people (a quarter of the population) were wounded, and today approximately 350,000 people remain displaced, the majority of them Christian Lebanese who were forced out of the Chouf mountains.
Palestine	Palestine (Greek: Παλαιστ?νη, Palaistine; Latin: Palaestina; Hebrew: ????????? Eretz-Yisra'el, (formerly also ????????, Palestina); Arabic: ??????? Filas?in, Falas?in, Filis?in) is a conventional name used, among others, to describe a geographic region between the Mediterranean Sea and the Jordan River, and various adjoining lands.
	Other terms for the same area include Canaan, Zion, the Land of Israel, and the Holy Land. Southern Levant is another purely geographic term, often implemented for the region, which does not have political or theologic implications.
Syria	Syria, officially the Syrian Arab Republic, is a country in Western Asia, bordering Lebanon and the Mediterranean Sea to the West, Turkey to the north, Iraq to the east, Jordan to the south, and Israel to the southwest.
	The name Syria formerly comprised the entire region of the Levant, while the modern state encompasses the site of several ancient kingdoms and empires, including the Eblan civilization of the third millennium BC. In the Islamic era, its capital city, Damascus, was the seat of the Umayyad Empire and a provincial capital of the Mamluk Empire. Damascus is one of the oldest continuously inhabited cities in the world.
Arabia	Arabia was a satrapy (province) of the Achaemenid Empire and later of the Sassanid Empire, by the name of Arabistan.
	Achaemenid Era

Achaemenid Arabia corresponded to the lands between Egypt and Mesopotamia, known as Arabia Petraea. According to Herodotus, the Cambyses did not subdue the Arabs when he attacked Egypt in 525 BCE. His successor Darius the Great does not mention the Arabs in the Behistun inscription from the first years of his reign, but mentions them in later texts.

| Damascus | Damascus is the capital and the second largest city of Syria as well as one of the country's 14 governorates. The Damascus Governorate is ruled by a governor appointed by the Minister of Interior. In addition to being the oldest continuously inhabited city in the world, Damascus is a major cultural and religious center of the Levant. |

| Emir | Emir, ("commander" or "general", also "prince" ; also transliterated as amir, aamir or ameer) is a high title of nobility or office, used throughout the Muslim world. Emirs are usually considered high-ranking sheikhs, but in monarchical states the term is also used for princes, with "Emirate" being analogous to principality in this sense.

While emir is the predominant spelling in English and many other languages, amir, closer to the original Arabic, is more common for its numerous compounds (e.g. admiral) and in individual names. |

| Saudi Arabia | The Kingdom of Saudi Arabia, commonly known as Saudi Arabia is, in land area, the third largest Arab country and the largest country in the Middle East. It is bordered by Jordan and Iraq on the north and northeast, Kuwait, Qatar and the United Arab Emirates on the east, Oman on the southeast, and Yemen on the south. It is also connected to Bahrain by the King Fahd Causeway. |

| Emunim | Emunim is a moshav in central Israel. Located near Ashdod, it falls under the jurisdiction of Be'er Tuvia Regional Council. In 2006 it had a population of 732

The moshav was founded in 1950 by immigrants from Egypt, on the land of the Palestinian village of Beit Daras. |

241

CIam101

Chapter 9. LEBANON, THE WEST BANK, AND THE CAMP DAVID ACCORDS

Husayn	Husayn is an Arabic name which is the diminutive of Hassan, meaning "good", "handsome" or "beautiful". It is commonly given as a male given name among Muslims, in honor of Husayn ibn Ali (626-680 AD). In some Persian sources the forms ?osayn, Hosayn, or Hossein is used.
Iraq	Iraq ; officially the Republic of Iraq is a country in Western Asia spanning most of the northwestern end of the Zagros mountain range, the eastern part of the Syrian Desert and the northern part of the Arabian Desert. Iraq is bordered by Jordan to the west, Syria to the northwest, Turkey to the north, Iran to the east, and Kuwait and Saudi Arabia to the south. Iraq has a narrow section of coastline measuring 58 km (35 miles) on the northern Persian Gulf.
Kuwait	The State of Kuwait is a sovereign Arab nation situated in the northeast of the Arabian Peninsula in Western Asia. It is bordered by Saudi Arabia to the south, and Iraq to the north. It lies on the northwestern shore of the Persian Gulf.
Ariel	Ariel is an Israeli settlement and a city in the central West Bank. Established in 1978, its population at the end of 2009 was 17,600, including 7,000 immigrants who came to Israel after 1990. It is the fourth largest Jewish settlement city in the West Bank., after Modi'in Illit, Beitar Illit, and Ma'ale Adumim. In Hebrew, Ariel, literally means 'Lion of God'.
Cold War	Cold War is a video game developed by Czech developer Mindware Studios and published by DreamCatcher Games (Linux Game Publishing for Linux). The game is similar to the Splinter Cell series of games in that it uses a stealth-action system of gameplay. The game distinguishes itself by adding an invention system where the player can use seemingly useless objects to create tools and weapons.
West Bank	The West Bank of the Jordan River is the landlocked geographical eastern part of the Palestinian territories located in the Western Asia. To the west, north, and south, the West Bank shares borders with the state of Israel. To the east, across the Jordan River, lies the Hashemite Kingdom of Jordan.

Chapter 9. LEBANON, THE WEST BANK, AND THE CAMP DAVID ACCORDS

Aqaba	Aqaba is a coastal town in the far south of Jordan. It is the capital of Aqaba Governorate. Aqaba is strategically important to Jordan as it is the country's only seaport.
Judea	35°18′23″E? / ?31.69889°N 35.30639°E

Judea, when Roman Judea was renamed Syria Palaestina following the Jewish Bar Kokhba revolt.

Etymology

The name Judea is a Greek and Roman adaptation of the name "Judah", which originally encompassed the territory of the Israelite tribe of that name and later of the ancient Kingdom of Judah. It was the name in use in English throughout history until the Jordanian occupation of the area.

Orthodox

Orthodox Basketball Club formerly known as Fastlink Basketball Club is a Jordanian basketball club based in Amman, Jordan. They compete in the Jordanian Basketball Federation.

Tournament records

WABA Champions Cup

- 1999: Champions
- 2001: 2nd place
- 2002: 2nd place
- 2004: 1st place
- 2008: 2nd place
- 2009: 1st place

Asia Champions Cup

- 1988: 5th place
- 1996: 7th place
- 1999: 6th place

245

Chapter 9. LEBANON, THE WEST BANK, AND THE CAMP DAVID ACCORDS

Samaria	Samaria is a term used for a mountainous region roughly corresponding to the northern part of the West Bank. According to 1 Kings 16:24, it is derived from the individual [or clan] Shemer, from whom Omri purchased the site. The name was the only name used for this area from ancient times until the Jordanian conquest of 1948, at which point the Jordanian occupiers coined the term West Bank.
Sharm el-Sheikh	Sharm el-Sheikh is a city situated on the southern tip of the Sinai Peninsula, in South Sinai Governorate, Egypt, on the coastal strip along the Red Sea with a population of approximately 35,000 (2008). Sharm el-Sheikh is the administrative hub of Egypt's South Sinai Governorate which includes the smaller coastal towns of Dahab and Nuweiba as well as the mountainous interior, Saint Catherine's Monastery and Mount Sinai. Name Sharm el-Sheikh is sometimes called the "City of Peace", referring to the large number of international peace conferences that have been held there.
Correspondence	In theology, correspondence is the relationship between spiritual and natural realities, or between mental and physical realities. The term was coined by the 18th century theologian Emanuel Swedenborg in his Arcana Coelestia (1749-1756) and Heaven and Hell (1758) and other works. Swedenborg states that there is a correspondence between, for example: thought and speech, between intention and action, between mind and body, and between God and creation.
Hama	Hama is a city on the banks of the Orontes River in central Syria north of Damascus. It is the provincial capital of the Hama Governorate. The city is the location of the historical city Hamath.

Chapter 9. LEBANON, THE WEST BANK, AND THE CAMP DAVID ACCORDS

Zionism	Zionism is a Jewish political movement that, in its broadest sense, has supported the self-determination of the Jewish people in a sovereign Jewish national homeland. Since the establishment of the State of Israel, the Zionist movement continues primarily to advocate on behalf of the Jewish state and address threats to its continued existence and security. In a less common usage, the term may also refer to 1) non-political, Cultural Zionism, founded and represented most prominently by Ahad Ha'am; and 2) political support for the State of Israel by non-Jews, as in Christian Zionism.
Response	A response is the second half of one of a set of preces, the said or sung answer by the congregation or choir to a versicle said or sung by an officiant or cantor. In the following opening of the Anglican service of Evening Prayer according to the Book of Common Prayer (BCP), the first line is the versicle and the second is the response. In some liturgical books (such as hymnals or breviaries) the symbol "R/" or "?" is used to denote a response.
Sharif	Sharif or Chérif is a traditional Arab tribal title given to those who serve as the protector of the tribe and all tribal assets, such as property, wells, and land. In origin, the word is an adjective meaning "noble", "highborn". The feminine singular is sharifa(h) (.
Alexander	Alexander, son of Perseus of Macedon, was a child at the conquest of his father by the Romans, and after the triumph of Aemilus Paullus in 167 BC, was kept in custody at Alba Fucens, together with his father. He became skilful in the toreutic art, learned the Latin language, and became a public notary.
Anwar	Anwar is the English transliteration of two Arabic names commonly used in the Muslim world: the male given name Anwar meaning "luminous" or the female given name Anwar (??????????), meaning "a collection of lights." Both names may also be encountered as surnames. In francophone countries, both names are usually transliterated as Anouar. The name is transliterated in Albania, Bosnia and Turkey as Enver.
Assassination	An assassination is "to murder (a usually prominent person) by a sudden and/or secret attack, often for political reasons." An additional definition is "the act of deliberately killing someone especially a public figure, usually for hire or for political reasons."

Assassinations may be prompted by religious, ideological, political, or military motives. Additionally, assassins may be prompted by financial gain, revenge for perceived grievances, a desire to acquire fame or notoriety (that is, a psychological need to garner personal public recognition), a wish to form some kind of "relationship" with the public figure, a wish or at least willingness to be killed or commit suicide in the attack.

Etymology

The word assassin is derived from the word Hashshashin, and shares its etymological roots with hashish .

Abdullah	Abdullah is a common Arabic male name. Humility before Allah is an essential value of Islam, hence Abdullah is a favorite name among Muslims. It was once common among Arabic-speaking Jews as well, especially Iraqi Jews.
Mubarak	Mubarak is an Arabic given name, which has the meaning "blessed one". A variant form is Barak or Barack, not to be confused with the unrelated Hebrew name Baraq; also anglicized as "Barak" or "Barack"). Mubarak and Barack are thus the Arabic equivalent in meaning of the Latinate "Benedict" .
Transjordan	The Transjordan is a section of the land of Israel mentioned in the Hebrew Bible. It is the land east of the Jordan River in which the tribes of Reuben and Gad, and half the tribe of Manasseh settle. Name The prefix trans- is Latin and means "across" or beyond, and so "Transjordan" refers to the land on the other side of the Jordan River.
Alliance	This article incorporates text from Easton's Bible Dictionary (1897), a publication now in the public domain.

Chapter 9. LEBANON, THE WEST BANK, AND THE CAMP DAVID ACCORDS

Abraham formed an alliance with some of the Canaanitish princes (Gen. 14:13), also with Abimelech (21:22-32). Joshua and the elders of Israel entered into an alliance with the Gibeonites (Josh. 9:3-27). When the Israelites entered Canaan they were forbidden to enter into alliances with the inhabitants of the country (Lev. 18:3, 4; 20:22, 23).

Arab

The proper name Arab or "Arabian" (and cognates in other languages) has been used to translate several different but similar sounding words in ancient and classical texts which do not necessarily have the same meaning or origin. Grunebaum, in his book Classical Islam said that an approximate translation is "passerby" or "nomad". Will Durant, in The Age of Faith, said that Arab meant Arid.

Ashkenazi Jews

Ashkenazi Jews, are the Jews descended from the medieval Jewish communities along the Rhine in Germany from Alsace in the south to the Rhineland in the north. Ashkenaz is the medieval Hebrew name for this region and thus for Germany. Thus, Ashkenazim or Ashkenazi Jews are literally "German Jews." Later, Jews from Western and Central Europe came to be called "Ashkenaz" because the main centers of Jewish learning were located in Germany.

Libya

Libya was a satrapy of the Achaemenid Empire according to King Darius I of Persia Naqshe Rustam and King Xerxes I of Persia' Daiva inscription. It is also mentioned as being part of the 6th district by Herodotus, which also included Cyrene, a Greek colony in Libya. When King Cambyses II of Persia conquered Egypt, the king of Cyrene, Arcesilaus III, sided with Persia.

Laws

The Laws is Plato's last and longest dialogue. The question asked at the beginning is not "What is law?" as one would expect. That is the question of the (pseudo?)Platonic Minos.

World

WORLD Magazine is a biweekly Christian news magazine, published in the United States of America by God's World Publications, a non-profit 501(c)(3) organization based in Asheville, North Carolina. WORLD differs from most other news magazines in that its declared perspective is one of conservative evangelical Protestantism. Its mission statement is "To report, interpret, and illustrate the news in a timely, accurate, enjoyable, and arresting fashion from a perspective committed to the Bible as the inerrant Word of God."

Each issue features both U.S. and international news, cultural analysis, editorials and commentary, as well as book, music and movie reviews.

Chapter 9. LEBANON, THE WEST BANK, AND THE CAMP DAVID ACCORDS

Arafat	Arafat is a surname or given name, and may refer to:
	• Yasser Arafat
	• Fathi Arafat Palestinian physician
	• Moussa Arafat cousin of Yasser Arafat
	• Raed Arafat Romanian physician
	• Suha Arafat widow of Yasser Arafat
	• Yasir Arafat , Pakistani cricketer
Christian	A Christian is a person who adheres to Christianity, an Abrahamic, monotheistic religion based on the life and teachings of Jesus of Nazareth as recorded in the Canonical gospels and the letters of the New Testament.
	Central to the Christian faith is love or Agape. Christians also believe Jesus is the Messiah prophesied in the Hebrew Bible, the Son of God, and the savior of mankind from their sins.
Amin	Amin is a male Arabic, Persian and Indian given name that means "faithful, trustworthy". Alternatives include Ameen and Amien.
	The female equivalent of Amin is Amina.
Barak	Barak, Al-Buraq the son of Abinoam from Kedesh in Naphtali, was a military general in the Book of Judges in the Bible. He was the commander of the army of Deborah, the prophetess and heroine of the Hebrew Bible. Barak and Deborah are credited with defeating the Canaanite armies led by Sisera, who for twenty years had oppressed the Israelites.
Ehud	Ehud ben-Gera is described in the Biblical Book of Judges as a judge who was sent by God to deliver the Israelites from the Moabite yoke.

CIam101

Ehud was sent to the Moabite King Eglon on the pretext of delivering the Israelites' annual tribute. He had blacksmiths make a double-edged shortsword about eighteen inches long, useful for a stabbing thrust.

Chapter 10. FROM PARIAH TO PARTNER

Egypt	The Roman province of Egypt was established in 30 BC after Octavian (the future emperor Augustus) defeated his rival Mark Antony, deposed his lover Queen Cleopatra VII and annexed the Ptolemaic kingdom of Egypt to the Roman Empire. The province encompassed most of modern-day Egypt except for the Sinai Peninsula (which would later be conquered by Trajan). Aegyptus was bordered by the provinces of Creta et Cyrenaica to the West and Judaea to the East.
Syria	Syria, officially the Syrian Arab Republic, is a country in Western Asia, bordering Lebanon and the Mediterranean Sea to the West, Turkey to the north, Iraq to the east, Jordan to the south, and Israel to the southwest. The name Syria formerly comprised the entire region of the Levant, while the modern state encompasses the site of several ancient kingdoms and empires, including the Eblan civilization of the third millennium BC. In the Islamic era, its capital city, Damascus, was the seat of the Umayyad Empire and a provincial capital of the Mamluk Empire. Damascus is one of the oldest continuously inhabited cities in the world.
Republic	Republic is a Hungarian rock band formed in Budapest in 1989. Their style is a unique mix of Western rock music and traditional Hungarian folk music. The band is popular in its native country and among Hungarian speaking minorities elsewhere. Members The two founding members are László Bódi and Lászlo Attila Nagy.
Cold War	Cold War is a video game developed by Czech developer Mindware Studios and published by DreamCatcher Games (Linux Game Publishing for Linux). The game is similar to the Splinter Cell series of games in that it uses a stealth-action system of gameplay. The game distinguishes itself by adding an invention system where the player can use seemingly useless objects to create tools and weapons.
Hama	Hama is a city on the banks of the Orontes River in central Syria north of Damascus. It is the provincial capital of the Hama Governorate. The city is the location of the historical city Hamath.

Chapter 10. FROM PARIAH TO PARTNER

Hebron	Hebron, is located in the southern West Bank, 30 km (19 mi) south of Jerusalem. Nestled in the Judean Mountains, it lies 930 meters (3,050 ft) above sea level. It is the largest city in the West Bank and home to around 165,000 Palestinians, and over 500 Jewish settlers concentrated in and around the old quarter.
Husayn	Husayn is an Arabic name which is the diminutive of Hassan, meaning "good", "handsome" or "beautiful". It is commonly given as a male given name among Muslims, in honor of Husayn ibn Ali (626-680 AD). In some Persian sources the forms ?osayn, Hosayn, or Hossein is used.
Kuwait	The State of Kuwait is a sovereign Arab nation situated in the northeast of the Arabian Peninsula in Western Asia. It is bordered by Saudi Arabia to the south, and Iraq to the north. It lies on the northwestern shore of the Persian Gulf.
Palestine	Palestine (Greek: Παλαιστ?νη, Palaistine; Latin: Palaestina; Hebrew: ????????? Eretz-Yisra'el, (formerly also ????????, Palestina); Arabic: ??????? Filas?in, Falas?in, Filis?in) is a conventional name used, among others, to describe a geographic region between the Mediterranean Sea and the Jordan River, and various adjoining lands. Other terms for the same area include Canaan, Zion, the Land of Israel, and the Holy Land. Southern Levant is another purely geographic term, often implemented for the region, which does not have political or theologic implications.
Politics	Aristotle's Politics is a work of political philosophy. The end of the Nicomachean Ethics declared that the inquiry into ethics necessarily follows into politics, and the two works are frequently considered to be parts of a larger treatise, or perhaps connected lectures, dealing with the "philosophy of human affairs." The title of the Politics literally means "the things concerning the polis." Composition

Chapter 10. FROM PARIAH TO PARTNER

The literary character of the Politics is subject to some dispute, growing out of the textual difficulties that attended the loss of Aristotle's works. Book III ends with a sentence that is repeated almost verbatim at the start of Book VII, while the intervening Books IV-VI seem to have a very different flavor from the rest; Book IV seems to refer several times back to the discussion of the best regime contained in Books VII-VIII. Some editors have therefore inserted Books VII-VIII after Book III. At the same time, however, references to the "discourses on politics" that occur in the Nicomachean Ethics suggest that the treatise as a whole ought to conclude with the discussion of education that occurs in Book VIII of the Politics, although it is not certain that Aristotle is referring to the Politics here.

Aqaba	Aqaba is a coastal town in the far south of Jordan. It is the capital of Aqaba Governorate. Aqaba is strategically important to Jordan as it is the country's only seaport.
Libya	Libya was a satrapy of the Achaemenid Empire according to King Darius I of Persia Naqshe Rustam and King Xerxes I of Persia' Daiva inscription. It is also mentioned as being part of the 6th district by Herodotus, which also included Cyrene, a Greek colony in Libya. When King Cambyses II of Persia conquered Egypt, the king of Cyrene, Arcesilaus III, sided with Persia.
Sharif	Sharif or Chérif is a traditional Arab tribal title given to those who serve as the protector of the tribe and all tribal assets, such as property, wells, and land. In origin, the word is an adjective meaning "noble", "highborn". The feminine singular is sharifa(h) (.
Sharm el-Sheikh	Sharm el-Sheikh is a city situated on the southern tip of the Sinai Peninsula, in South Sinai Governorate, Egypt, on the coastal strip along the Red Sea with a population of approximately 35,000 (2008). Sharm el-Sheikh is the administrative hub of Egypt's South Sinai Governorate which includes the smaller coastal towns of Dahab and Nuweiba as well as the mountainous interior, Saint Catherine's Monastery and Mount Sinai.
	Name
	Sharm el-Sheikh is sometimes called the "City of Peace", referring to the large number of international peace conferences that have been held there.

Chapter 10. FROM PARIAH TO PARTNER

West Bank	The West Bank of the Jordan River is the landlocked geographical eastern part of the Palestinian territories located in the Western Asia. To the west, north, and south, the West Bank shares borders with the state of Israel. To the east, across the Jordan River, lies the Hashemite Kingdom of Jordan.
State	The term state is used in various senses by Catholic theologians and spiritual writers. It may be taken to signify a profession or calling in life, as where St. Paul says, in I Corinthians 7:20: "Let every man abide in the same calling in which he was called". States are classified in the Catholic Church as the clerical state, the religious state, and the secular state; and among religious states, again, we have those of the contemplative, the active, and the mixed orders.
Arab	The proper name Arab or "Arabian" (and cognates in other languages) has been used to translate several different but similar sounding words in ancient and classical texts which do not necessarily have the same meaning or origin. Grunebaum, in his book Classical Islam said that an approximate translation is "passerby" or "nomad". Will Durant, in The Age of Faith, said that Arab meant Arid.
Baghdad	Baghdad is the capital of Iraq, as well as the coterminous Baghdad Governorate. With an estimated population between 7 and 7.5 million, it is the largest city in Iraq, the second largest city in the Arab World (after Cairo, Egypt), and the second largest city in Western Asia (after Tehran, Iran). Located along the Tigris River, the city was founded in the 8th century and became the capital of the Abbasid Caliphate.
Emir	Emir, ("commander" or "general", also "prince" ; also transliterated as amir, aamir or ameer) is a high title of nobility or office, used throughout the Muslim world. Emirs are usually considered high-ranking sheikhs, but in monarchical states the term is also used for princes, with "Emirate" being analogous to principality in this sense.

While emir is the predominant spelling in English and many other languages, amir, closer to the original Arabic, is more common for its numerous compounds (e.g. admiral) and in individual names.

Difference	Difference is a key concept of continental philosophy, opposed to Identity. Gilles Deleuze's Difference and Repetition (1968) was an attempt, to think Difference as having an ontological privilege over Identity, inversing the traditional relationship between those two concepts.
Peace	Peace is an Athenian Old Comedy written and produced by the Greek playwright Aristophanes. It won second prize at the City Dionysia where it was staged just a few days before the ratification of the Peace of Nicias (421 BC), which promised to end the ten year old Peloponnesian War. The play is notable for its joyous anticipation of peace and for its celebration of a return to an idyllic life in the countryside.
Arab nationalism	Arab nationalism is a nationalist ideology celebrating the glories of Arab civilization, the language and literature of the Arabs, calling for rejuvenation and political union in the Arab world. Its central premise is that the peoples of the Arab World, from the Atlantic Ocean to the Arabian Sea, constitute one nation bound together by common linguistic, cultural, religious, and historical heritage, One of the primary goals of Arab nationalism is the end of Western influence in the Arab World, seen as a "nemesis" of Arab strength, and the removal of those Arab governments considered to be dependent upon Western power. It rose to prominence with the weakening and defeat of the Ottoman Empire in the early 20th century and declined after the defeat of the Arab armies in the Six Day War.
Front	Front was first published by Cabal Communications in 1998, it was created to rival IPC's publication Loaded, catering to a demographic of 16-25 year-old males. It began as part of the British "lads' mag" genre of magazines though the covers rejects this description with the statement "Front is no lads' mag".

Whilst a major selling point is the photo-shoots of models, the magazine also focuses heavily on music, films, gadgets and games, plus sections on fashion and sport.

Mubarak

Mubarak is an Arabic given name, which has the meaning "blessed one". A variant form is Barak or Barack, not to be confused with the unrelated Hebrew name Baraq; also anglicized as "Barak" or "Barack"). Mubarak and Barack are thus the Arabic equivalent in meaning of the Latinate "Benedict" .

India

India was an ecclesiastical province of the Church of the East, at least nominally, from the seventh to the sixteenth century. The Malabar Coast of India had long been home to a thriving East Syrian (Nestorian) Christian community, known as the St. Thomas Christians. The community traces its origins to the evangelical activity of Thomas the Apostle in the 1st century.

Israeli settlement

An Israeli settlement is an Israeli civilian community on land that was captured by Israel during the Six-Day War and is considered by the international community (excluding Israel) to be occupied territory. Such settlements currently exist in the West Bank, East Jerusalem, and the Golan Heights.

The International Court of Justice and the international community say these settlements are illegal,.

Impact

Impact is a monthly magazine published in the United Kingdom. It covers the field of action entertainment: including Hong Kong action cinema, worldwide martial arts films, Hollywood productions, anime, comics, action films and East Asian cinema in general. Originally founded and edited by Bey Logan, it is presently edited by John Mosby, with Mike Leeder acting as Eastern Editor from the Hong Kong office, and Andrez Bergen as Tokyo Correspondent.

Lebanon

Lebanon is a mural size painting by Nabil Kanso depicting the Lebanese Civil War in a scene invoking the spirit and character of the people in the midst of horror and violence gripping the country. Amid the scene of chaos and devastation, two central figures reach across toward each other symbolically to represent the appeal for unity in defiance of the forces of division, destruction, and terror.

Description

	Painted in oil on linen and completed in 1983, the painting Lebanon measures 28 feet (8.5 meters) long by 10 feet (3meters) tall.
Ahmad	Ahmad and Ahmed are the principal transliterations of the Arabic given name . The latter name comes from the Arabic triconsonantal root of ?-M-D, meaning "highly praised", implying "one who constantly thanks Allah". Etymology One of the Islamic prophet Muhammad's many names is Ahmad, the name "Muhammad" pre-dating "Ahmad".
Mandate	In Christian theology, a mandate is an order given from God that must be obeyed without question. For example, the mandate given to Abraham to offer his son Isaac as a sacrifice to God. (Genesis 22:1)
Shaykh Ahmad	Shaykh Ahmad ibn Zayn al-Dín ibn Ibráhím al-Ahsá'í was (1753 - 1826) was the founder of a 19th century Shi`i school in the Persian and Ottoman empires, whose followers are known as Shaykhís. He was a native of the Al-Ahsa region, educated in Bahrain and the theological centers of Najaf and Karbala in Iraq. Spending the last twenty years of his life in Iran, he received the protection and patronage of princes of the Qajar dynasty.
Zionism	Zionism is a Jewish political movement that, in its broadest sense, has supported the self-determination of the Jewish people in a sovereign Jewish national homeland. Since the establishment of the State of Israel, the Zionist movement continues primarily to advocate on behalf of the Jewish state and address threats to its continued existence and security. In a less common usage, the term may also refer to 1) non-political, Cultural Zionism, founded and represented most prominently by Ahad Ha'am; and 2) political support for the State of Israel by non-Jews, as in Christian Zionism.

Response	A response is the second half of one of a set of preces, the said or sung answer by the congregation or choir to a versicle said or sung by an officiant or cantor. In the following opening of the Anglican service of Evening Prayer according to the Book of Common Prayer (BCP), the first line is the versicle and the second is the response. In some liturgical books (such as hymnals or breviaries) the symbol "R/" or "?" is used to denote a response.
Judea	35°18′23″E? / ?31.69889°N 35.30639°E Judea, when Roman Judea was renamed Syria Palaestina following the Jewish Bar Kokhba revolt. Etymology The name Judea is a Greek and Roman adaptation of the name "Judah", which originally encompassed the territory of the Israelite tribe of that name and later of the ancient Kingdom of Judah. It was the name in use in English throughout history until the Jordanian occupation of the area.
Samaria	Samaria is a term used for a mountainous region roughly corresponding to the northern part of the West Bank. According to 1 Kings 16:24, it is derived from the individual [or clan] Shemer, from whom Omri purchased the site. The name was the only name used for this area from ancient times until the Jordanian conquest of 1948, at which point the Jordanian occupiers coined the term West Bank.
Abbasid Caliphate	The Abbasid caliphate, more simply, the Abbasids, was the third of the Islamic caliphates. It was ruled by the Abbasid dynasty of caliphs, who built their capital in Baghdad after overthrowing the Umayyad caliphs from all but the Al Andalus region.

Chapter 10. FROM PARIAH TO PARTNER

	The Abbasid caliphate was founded by the descendants of the Islamic prophet Muhammad's youngest uncle, Abbas ibn Abd al-Muttalib, in Harran in 750 CE and shifted its capital in 762 to Baghdad.
Caliphate	The term caliphate "dominion of a caliph ('successor,')," refers to the first system of government established in Islam, and represented the political unity of the Muslim Ummah (nation). In theory, it is a constitutional republic , meaning that the head of state (the Caliph) and other officials are dicate to the people according to Islamic law, which exercises power over their citizens. It was initially led by Muhammad's disciples as a continuation of the political system the prophet established, known as the 'rashidun caliphates'.
Iraq	Iraq ; officially the Republic of Iraq is a country in Western Asia spanning most of the northwestern end of the Zagros mountain range, the eastern part of the Syrian Desert and the northern part of the Arabian Desert. Iraq is bordered by Jordan to the west, Syria to the northwest, Turkey to the north, Iran to the east, and Kuwait and Saudi Arabia to the south. Iraq has a narrow section of coastline measuring 58 km (35 miles) on the northern Persian Gulf.
Abbas	Abbas means "lion" in Arabic. (Austere: (1) severely simple in appearance. (2) strict, stern).
Arabia	Arabia was a satrapy (province) of the Achaemenid Empire and later of the Sassanid Empire, by the name of Arabistan. Achaemenid Era Achaemenid Arabia corresponded to the lands between Egypt and Mesopotamia, known as Arabia Petraea. According to Herodotus, the Cambyses did not subdue the Arabs when he attacked Egypt in 525 BCE. His successor Darius the Great does not mention the Arabs in the Behistun inscription from the first years of his reign, but mentions them in later texts.

275

Chapter 10. FROM PARIAH TO PARTNER

Saudi Arabia	The Kingdom of Saudi Arabia, commonly known as Saudi Arabia is, in land area, the third largest Arab country and the largest country in the Middle East. It is bordered by Jordan and Iraq on the north and northeast, Kuwait, Qatar and the United Arab Emirates on the east, Oman on the southeast, and Yemen on the south. It is also connected to Bahrain by the King Fahd Causeway.
World	WORLD Magazine is a biweekly Christian news magazine, published in the United States of America by God's World Publications, a non-profit 501(c)(3) organization based in Asheville, North Carolina. WORLD differs from most other news magazines in that its declared perspective is one of conservative evangelical Protestantism. Its mission statement is "To report, interpret, and illustrate the news in a timely, accurate, enjoyable, and arresting fashion from a perspective committed to the Bible as the inerrant Word of God." Each issue features both U.S. and international news, cultural analysis, editorials and commentary, as well as book, music and movie reviews.
Prime	Prime, is a fixed time of prayer of the traditional Divine Office (Canonical Hours), said at the first hour of daylight (approximately 6:00 a.m)., between the morning Hour of Lauds and the 9 a.m. Hour of Terce. It is part of the Christian liturgies of Eastern Christianity, but in the Latin Rite it was suppressed by the Second Vatican Council. However, clergy who have an obligation to celebrate the Liturgy of the Hours may still fulfil their obligation by using the Roman Breviary promulgated by Pope John XXIII in 1962, which contains the Hour of Prime.
Assassination	An assassination is "to murder (a usually prominent person) by a sudden and/or secret attack, often for political reasons." An additional definition is "the act of deliberately killing someone especially a public figure, usually for hire or for political reasons." Assassinations may be prompted by religious, ideological, political, or military motives. Additionally, assassins may be prompted by financial gain, revenge for perceived grievances, a desire to acquire fame or notoriety (that is, a psychological need to garner personal public recognition), a wish to form some kind of "relationship" with the public figure, a wish or at least willingness to be killed or commit suicide in the attack. Etymology

Chapter 10. FROM PARIAH TO PARTNER

The word assassin is derived from the word Hashshashin, and shares its etymological roots with hashish .

Emunim

Emunim is a moshav in central Israel. Located near Ashdod, it falls under the jurisdiction of Be'er Tuvia Regional Council. In 2006 it had a population of 732

The moshav was founded in 1950 by immigrants from Egypt, on the land of the Palestinian village of Beit Daras.

State

The term state is used in various senses by Catholic theologians and spiritual writers.

It may be taken to signify a profession or calling in life, as where St. Paul says, in I Corinthians 7:20: "Let every man abide in the same calling in which he was called". States are classified in the Catholic Church as the clerical state, the religious state, and the secular state; and among religious states, again, we have those of the contemplative, the active, and the mixed orders.

Chapter 11. ISRAELI-PALESTINIAN/ARAB NEGOTIATIONS AND AGREEMENTS, 1993-1999

Ariel	Ariel is an Israeli settlement and a city in the central West Bank. Established in 1978, its population at the end of 2009 was 17,600, including 7,000 immigrants who came to Israel after 1990. It is the fourth largest Jewish settlement city in the West Bank., after Modi'in Illit, Beitar Illit, and Ma'ale Adumim. In Hebrew, Ariel, literally means 'Lion of God'.
Barak	Barak, Al-Buraq the son of Abinoam from Kedesh in Naphtali, was a military general in the Book of Judges in the Bible. He was the commander of the army of Deborah, the prophetess and heroine of the Hebrew Bible. Barak and Deborah are credited with defeating the Canaanite armies led by Sisera, who for twenty years had oppressed the Israelites.
Cold War	Cold War is a video game developed by Czech developer Mindware Studios and published by DreamCatcher Games (Linux Game Publishing for Linux). The game is similar to the Splinter Cell series of games in that it uses a stealth-action system of gameplay. The game distinguishes itself by adding an invention system where the player can use seemingly useless objects to create tools and weapons.
Ehud	Ehud ben-Gera is described in the Biblical Book of Judges as a judge who was sent by God to deliver the Israelites from the Moabite yoke. Ehud was sent to the Moabite King Eglon on the pretext of delivering the Israelites' annual tribute. He had blacksmiths make a double-edged shortsword about eighteen inches long, useful for a stabbing thrust.
West Bank	The West Bank of the Jordan River is the landlocked geographical eastern part of the Palestinian territories located in the Western Asia. To the west, north, and south, the West Bank shares borders with the state of Israel. To the east, across the Jordan River, lies the Hashemite Kingdom of Jordan.
Assassination	An assassination is "to murder (a usually prominent person) by a sudden and/or secret attack, often for political reasons." An additional definition is "the act of deliberately killing someone especially a public figure, usually for hire or for political reasons."

Assassinations may be prompted by religious, ideological, political, or military motives. Additionally, assassins may be prompted by financial gain, revenge for perceived grievances, a desire to acquire fame or notoriety (that is, a psychological need to garner personal public recognition), a wish to form some kind of "relationship" with the public figure, a wish or at least willingness to be killed or commit suicide in the attack.

Etymology

The word assassin is derived from the word Hashshashin, and shares its etymological roots with hashish .

Prime

Prime, is a fixed time of prayer of the traditional Divine Office (Canonical Hours), said at the first hour of daylight (approximately 6:00 a.m)., between the morning Hour of Lauds and the 9 a.m. Hour of Terce. It is part of the Christian liturgies of Eastern Christianity, but in the Latin Rite it was suppressed by the Second Vatican Council. However, clergy who have an obligation to celebrate the Liturgy of the Hours may still fulfil their obligation by using the Roman Breviary promulgated by Pope John XXIII in 1962, which contains the Hour of Prime.

Mandate

In Christian theology, a mandate is an order given from God that must be obeyed without question. For example, the mandate given to Abraham to offer his son Isaac as a sacrifice to God. (Genesis 22:1)

Politics

Aristotle's Politics is a work of political philosophy. The end of the Nicomachean Ethics declared that the inquiry into ethics necessarily follows into politics, and the two works are frequently considered to be parts of a larger treatise, or perhaps connected lectures, dealing with the "philosophy of human affairs." The title of the Politics literally means "the things concerning the polis."

Composition

283

The literary character of the Politics is subject to some dispute, growing out of the textual difficulties that attended the loss of Aristotle's works. Book III ends with a sentence that is repeated almost verbatim at the start of Book VII, while the intervening Books IV-VI seem to have a very different flavor from the rest; Book IV seems to refer several times back to the discussion of the best regime contained in Books VII-VIII. Some editors have therefore inserted Books VII-VIII after Book III. At the same time, however, references to the "discourses on politics" that occur in the Nicomachean Ethics suggest that the treatise as a whole ought to conclude with the discussion of education that occurs in Book VIII of the Politics, although it is not certain that Aristotle is referring to the Politics here.

State	The term state is used in various senses by Catholic theologians and spiritual writers.
	It may be taken to signify a profession or calling in life, as where St. Paul says, in I Corinthians 7:20: "Let every man abide in the same calling in which he was called". States are classified in the Catholic Church as the clerical state, the religious state, and the secular state; and among religious states, again, we have those of the contemplative, the active, and the mixed orders.
Gush Etzion	Gush Etzion is a collection of Israeli settlements located in the occupied West Bank. The settlements were built following the 1967 Six-Day War, along with new settlements, that have expanded the area of the Etzion Bloc. Like other Israeli settlements established after 1967 in the occupied West Bank, they are considered illegal under international law by the international community, though Israel disputes this.
Hebron	Hebron, is located in the southern West Bank, 30 km (19 mi) south of Jerusalem. Nestled in the Judean Mountains, it lies 930 meters (3,050 ft) above sea level. It is the largest city in the West Bank and home to around 165,000 Palestinians, and over 500 Jewish settlers concentrated in and around the old quarter.
Israeli settlement	An Israeli settlement is an Israeli civilian community on land that was captured by Israel during the Six-Day War and is considered by the international community (excluding Israel) to be occupied territory. Such settlements currently exist in the West Bank, East Jerusalem, and the Golan Heights.

	The International Court of Justice and the international community say these settlements are illegal,.
Emunim	Emunim is a moshav in central Israel. Located near Ashdod, it falls under the jurisdiction of Be'er Tuvia Regional Council. In 2006 it had a population of 732
	The moshav was founded in 1950 by immigrants from Egypt, on the land of the Palestinian village of Beit Daras.
Husayn	Husayn is an Arabic name which is the diminutive of Hassan, meaning "good", "handsome" or "beautiful". It is commonly given as a male given name among Muslims, in honor of Husayn ibn Ali (626-680 AD). In some Persian sources the forms ?osayn, Hosayn, or Hossein is used.
Iraq	Iraq ; officially the Republic of Iraq is a country in Western Asia spanning most of the northwestern end of the Zagros mountain range, the eastern part of the Syrian Desert and the northern part of the Arabian Desert.
	Iraq is bordered by Jordan to the west, Syria to the northwest, Turkey to the north, Iran to the east, and Kuwait and Saudi Arabia to the south. Iraq has a narrow section of coastline measuring 58 km (35 miles) on the northern Persian Gulf.
Kuwait	The State of Kuwait is a sovereign Arab nation situated in the northeast of the Arabian Peninsula in Western Asia. It is bordered by Saudi Arabia to the south, and Iraq to the north. It lies on the northwestern shore of the Persian Gulf.
State	The term state is used in various senses by Catholic theologians and spiritual writers.

It may be taken to signify a profession or calling in life, as where St. Paul says, in I Corinthians 7:20: "Let every man abide in the same calling in which he was called". States are classified in the Catholic Church as the clerical state, the religious state, and the secular state; and among religious states, again, we have those of the contemplative, the active, and the mixed orders.

East Jerusalem

East Jerusalem refers to the parts of Jerusalem captured by Jordan in the 1948 Arab-Israeli War and then taken by Israel in the 1967 Six-Day War. It includes Jerusalem's Old City and some of the holiest sites of Judaism, Christianity, and Islam, such as the Temple Mount, Western Wall, Al-Aqsa Mosque, and the Church of the Holy Sepulchre. The term "East Jerusalem" may refer to either the area under Jordanian rule between 1949 and 1967 which was incorporated into the municipality of Jerusalem after 1967, covering some 70 km^2 (27 sq mi), or the territory of the pre-1967 Jordanian municipality, covering 6.4 km^2 (2.5 sq mi).

Jerusalem

Jerusalem [ii] is the capital of Israel, though not internationally recognized as such.[iii] If the area and population of East Jerusalem is included, it is Israel's largest city in both population and area, with a population of 763,800 residents over an area of 125.1 km^2 (48.3 sq mi).[iv] Located in the Judean Mountains, between the Mediterranean Sea and the northern edge of the Dead Sea, modern Jerusalem has grown far beyond the boundaries of the Old City.

Jerusalem is a holy city to the three major Abrahamic religions--Judaism, Christianity and Islam. In Judaism, Jerusalem has been the holiest city since, according to the Torah, King David of Israel first established it as the capital of the united Kingdom of Israel in c. 1000 BCE, and his son Solomon commissioned the building of the First Temple in the city.

Old City

The Old City is a 0.9 square kilometer (0.35 square mile) walled area within the modern city of Jerusalem. Until the 1860s this area constituted the entire city of Jerusalem. The Old City is home to several sites of key religious importance: the Temple Mount and its Western Wall for Jews, the Church of the Holy Sepulchre for Christians, and the Dome of the Rock and al-Aqsa Mosque for Muslims.

Palestine

Palestine (Greek: Παλαιστ?νη, Palaistine; Latin: Palaestina; Hebrew: ????????? Eretz-Yisra'el, (formerly also ????????, Palestina); Arabic: ??????? Filas?in, Falas?in, Filis?in) is a conventional name used, among others, to describe a geographic region between the Mediterranean Sea and the Jordan River, and various adjoining lands.

Other terms for the same area include Canaan, Zion, the Land of Israel, and the Holy Land. Southern Levant is another purely geographic term, often implemented for the region, which does not have political or theologic implications.

| Temple | In the Latter Day Saint movement, a temple is a building dedicated to be a house of God and is reserved for special forms of worship. A temple differs from a church meetinghouse, which is used for weekly worship services. Temples have been a significant part of the Latter Day Saint movement since early in its inception. |

Temple Mount

The Temple Mount, also known in the Bible as Mount Moriah (some also identify it with the biblical Mount Zion) and by Muslims as the Noble Sanctuary (Bait-ul-Muqaddas), is a religious site in the Old City of Jerusalem.

Judaism regards the Temple Mount as the place where God chose the Divine Presence to rest (Isa 8:18); it was from here the world expanded into its present form and where God gathered the dust used to create the first man, Adam.{According to the sages of the Talmud[13]} The site is the location of Abraham's binding of Isaac, and of two Jewish Temples. According to the Bible the site should function as the center of all national life - government, judicial and, of course, religious center (Deut 12:5-26; 14:23-25; 15:20; 16:2-16; 17:8-10; 26: 2; 31: 11; Isa 2: 2-5; Oba 1:21; Psa 48) .

Zionism

Zionism is a Jewish political movement that, in its broadest sense, has supported the self-determination of the Jewish people in a sovereign Jewish national homeland. Since the establishment of the State of Israel, the Zionist movement continues primarily to advocate on behalf of the Jewish state and address threats to its continued existence and security. In a less common usage, the term may also refer to 1) non-political, Cultural Zionism, founded and represented most prominently by Ahad Ha'am; and 2) political support for the State of Israel by non-Jews, as in Christian Zionism.

Response

A response is the second half of one of a set of preces, the said or sung answer by the congregation or choir to a versicle said or sung by an officiant or cantor. In the following opening of the Anglican service of Evening Prayer according to the Book of Common Prayer (BCP), the first line is the versicle and the second is the response.

	In some liturgical books (such as hymnals or breviaries) the symbol "R/" or "?" is used to denote a response.
Israeli settlement	An Israeli settlement is an Israeli civilian community on land that was captured by Israel during the Six-Day War and is considered by the international community (excluding Israel) to be occupied territory. Such settlements currently exist in the West Bank, East Jerusalem, and the Golan Heights. The International Court of Justice and the international community say these settlements are illegal,.
Judea	35°18′23″E? / ?31.69889°N 35.30639°E Judea, when Roman Judea was renamed Syria Palaestina following the Jewish Bar Kokhba revolt. Etymology The name Judea is a Greek and Roman adaptation of the name "Judah", which originally encompassed the territory of the Israelite tribe of that name and later of the ancient Kingdom of Judah. It was the name in use in English throughout history until the Jordanian occupation of the area.
Samaria	Samaria is a term used for a mountainous region roughly corresponding to the northern part of the West Bank. According to 1 Kings 16:24, it is derived from the individual [or clan] Shemer, from whom Omri purchased the site. The name was the only name used for this area from ancient times until the Jordanian conquest of 1948, at which point the Jordanian occupiers coined the term West Bank.
Hama	Hama is a city on the banks of the Orontes River in central Syria north of Damascus. It is the provincial capital of the Hama Governorate. The city is the location of the historical city Hamath.

293

Libya	Libya was a satrapy of the Achaemenid Empire according to King Darius I of Persia Naqshe Rustam and King Xerxes I of Persia' Daiva inscription. It is also mentioned as being part of the 6th district by Herodotus, which also included Cyrene, a Greek colony in Libya. When King Cambyses II of Persia conquered Egypt, the king of Cyrene, Arcesilaus III, sided with Persia.
Emir	Emir, ("commander" or "general", also "prince" ; also transliterated as amir, aamir or ameer) is a high title of nobility or office, used throughout the Muslim world. Emirs are usually considered high-ranking sheikhs, but in monarchical states the term is also used for princes, with "Emirate" being analogous to principality in this sense.
	While emir is the predominant spelling in English and many other languages, amir, closer to the original Arabic, is more common for its numerous compounds (e.g. admiral) and in individual names.
Syria	Syria, officially the Syrian Arab Republic, is a country in Western Asia, bordering Lebanon and the Mediterranean Sea to the West, Turkey to the north, Iraq to the east, Jordan to the south, and Israel to the southwest.
	The name Syria formerly comprised the entire region of the Levant, while the modern state encompasses the site of several ancient kingdoms and empires, including the Eblan civilization of the third millennium BC. In the Islamic era, its capital city, Damascus, was the seat of the Umayyad Empire and a provincial capital of the Mamluk Empire. Damascus is one of the oldest continuously inhabited cities in the world.
Commemoration	In the Roman Rite, when a higher-ranked liturgical celebration impedes the celebration of a lesser one that, either permanently or (in a particular year) by coincidence, falls on the same day, the prayer of the lower-ranked celebration is usually added to that of the higher. This additional prayer is referred to as a commemoration of the lesser celebration.
	In the post-Tridentine usage, on Sundays lacking the commemoration of a feast of Double rank, or of an Octave, a second and a third prayer was added to that of the Sunday.

295

Chapter 11. ISRAELI-PALESTINIAN/ARAB NEGOTIATIONS AND AGREEMENTS, 1993-1999

Peace	Peace is an Athenian Old Comedy written and produced by the Greek playwright Aristophanes. It won second prize at the City Dionysia where it was staged just a few days before the ratification of the Peace of Nicias (421 BC), which promised to end the ten year old Peloponnesian War. The play is notable for its joyous anticipation of peace and for its celebration of a return to an idyllic life in the countryside.
Alexander	Alexander, son of Perseus of Macedon, was a child at the conquest of his father by the Romans, and after the triumph of Aemilus Paullus in 167 BC, was kept in custody at Alba Fucens, together with his father. He became skilful in the toreutic art, learned the Latin language, and became a public notary.
Lebanon	Lebanon is a mural size painting by Nabil Kanso depicting the Lebanese Civil War in a scene invoking the spirit and character of the people in the midst of horror and violence gripping the country. Amid the scene of chaos and devastation, two central figures reach across toward each other symbolically to represent the appeal for unity in defiance of the forces of division, destruction, and terror.
	Description
	Painted in oil on linen and completed in 1983, the painting Lebanon measures 28 feet (8.5 meters) long by 10 feet (3meters) tall.

CLAM101

Chapter 11. ISRAELI-PALESTINIAN/ARAB NEGOTIATIONS AND AGREEMENTS, 1993-1999

Orthodox	Orthodox Basketball Club formerly known as Fastlink Basketball Club is a Jordanian basketball club based in Amman, Jordan. They compete in the Jordanian Basketball Federation.

Tournament records

WABA Champions Cup

- 1999: Champions
- 2001: 2nd place
- 2002: 2nd place
- 2004: 1st place
- 2008: 2nd place
- 2009: 1st place

Asia Champions Cup

- 1988: 5th place
- 1996: 7th place
- 1999: 6th place

. |
| Aqaba | Aqaba is a coastal town in the far south of Jordan. It is the capital of Aqaba Governorate. Aqaba is strategically important to Jordan as it is the country's only seaport. |
| Christian | A Christian is a person who adheres to Christianity, an Abrahamic, monotheistic religion based on the life and teachings of Jesus of Nazareth as recorded in the Canonical gospels and the letters of the New Testament.

Central to the Christian faith is love or Agape. Christians also believe Jesus is the Messiah prophesied in the Hebrew Bible, the Son of God, and the savior of mankind from their sins. |
| Labor Zionism | Labor Zionism can be described as the major stream of the left wing of the Zionist movement. It was, for many years, the most significant tendency among Zionists and Zionist organizational structure. It saw itself as the Zionist sector of the historic Jewish labor movements of Eastern and Central Europe, eventually developing local units in most countries with sizeable Jewish populations. |

Chapter 11. ISRAELI-PALESTINIAN/ARAB NEGOTIATIONS AND AGREEMENTS, 1993-1999

Revisionist Zionism	Revisionist Zionism is a nationalist faction within the Zionist movement. It is the founding ideology of the non-religious right in Israel, and was the chief ideological competitor to the dominant socialist Labor Zionism. Revisionism is represented primarily by the Likud Party.
Sharm el-Sheikh	Sharm el-Sheikh is a city situated on the southern tip of the Sinai Peninsula, in South Sinai Governorate, Egypt, on the coastal strip along the Red Sea with a population of approximately 35,000 (2008). Sharm el-Sheikh is the administrative hub of Egypt's South Sinai Governorate which includes the smaller coastal towns of Dahab and Nuweiba as well as the mountainous interior, Saint Catherine's Monastery and Mount Sinai. Name Sharm el-Sheikh is sometimes called the "City of Peace", referring to the large number of international peace conferences that have been held there.
Impact	Impact is a monthly magazine published in the United Kingdom. It covers the field of action entertainment: including Hong Kong action cinema, worldwide martial arts films, Hollywood productions, anime, comics, action films and East Asian cinema in general. Originally founded and edited by Bey Logan, it is presently edited by John Mosby, with Mike Leeder acting as Eastern Editor from the Hong Kong office, and Andrez Bergen as Tokyo Correspondent.

301

Amir	Amir is a given name and may refer to:

Given name

- Amir Persian pop singer
- Ameer Ali, Australian economist and community leader
- Ameer Bux Bhutto, Pakistani politician
- Ameer Bukhari, a Saudi student pilot
- Amir Derakh, American musician
- Abdul Ameer Yousef Habeeb, Iraqi journalist
- Amir Hamed, Uruguayan writer and translator
- Amir Hashemi, Iranian footballer
- Emir Isilay, Turkish musician
- Amir Karic, Bosnian-Slovenian footballer
- Amir Reza Khadem, Iranian wrestler
- Aamir Khan, Indian actor
- Amir Khan (boxer), English boxer
- Emir Kusturica, Yugoslavian filmmaker
- Amir Mohebi, Iranian footballer
- Amir Mokri, Iranian cinematographer
- Amir Nachumi, Israeli Air Force general
- Amir Naderi, Iranian film director
- Amir Peretz, Moroccan-born Israeli politician
- Amir Sadollah, American mixed martial artist
- Amir Slama, Brazilian fashion designer
- Amir Spahic, Bosnian footballer
- Ameer Sultan, a Tamil film director
- Amir Vahedi (1961-2010), Iranian-born American professional poker player

Surname

- Abdel Hakim Amer, Egyptian military commander during the Six-Day War
- Menashe Amir, a Persian language Israeli broadcaster
- Yigal Amir, the assassin of Prime Minister of Israel Yitzhak Rabin

Chapter 11. ISRAELI-PALESTINIAN/ARAB NEGOTIATIONS AND AGREEMENTS, 1993-1999

Yahya	Yahya ibn al-Mundhir al-Mudhaffar was the second boss of the Banu Tujibi group. He ruled Zaragoza from 1021-1029.
Caliph	The Caliph is the head of state in a Caliphate, and the title for the leader of the Islamic Ummah, an Islamic community ruled by the Shari'ah. It is a transcribed version of the Arabic word ????? Khalifah which means "successor" or "representative". Following Muhammad's death in 632, the early leaders of the Muslim nation were called "Khalifat Rasul Allah", the political successors to the messenger of God (referring to Muhammad).
Hasmoneans	The Hasmoneans were the ruling dynasty of the Hasmonean Kingdom of Israel (140-37 BCE), an independent religious Jewish state in the Land of Israel. The Hasmonean dynasty was established under the leadership of Simon Maccabaeus, two decades after his brother Judas the Maccabee ("Hammer") defeated the Seleucid army during the Maccabean Revolt in 165 BCE. The Hasmonean Kingdom survived for 103 years before yielding to the Herodian Dynasty in 37 BCE. Even then, Herod the Great felt obliged to bolster the legitimacy of his reign by marrying a Hasmonean princess, Mariamne, and conspiring to have the last male Hasmonean heir drowned in his Jericho palace.

According to historical sources including the books 1 Maccabees and 2 Maccabees and the first book of The Wars of the Jews by the Jewish historian Josephus (37-c. 100 CE), the Hasmonean Kingdom rose after a successful revolt by the Jews against the Seleucid king Antiochus IV. After Antiochus' successful invasion of Ptolemaic Egypt was turned back by the intervention of the Roman Republic he moved instead to assert strict control over Israel, sacking Jerusalem and its Temple, suppressing Jewish religious and cultural observances, and imposing Hellenistic practices. |
| Sharif | Sharif or Chérif is a traditional Arab tribal title given to those who serve as the protector of the tribe and all tribal assets, such as property, wells, and land. In origin, the word is an adjective meaning "noble", "highborn". The feminine singular is sharifa(h) (. |
| Tunnel | Tunnel is a nightclub in St. Petersburg, Russia, generally acknowledged to be the first techno club in the country when it opened in 1993. Located in a disused bomb shelter on Zverinskaya st, the club was shut down for an extended period of time but reopened in 2002 and is, as of December 2004, operating again in its original location. |

305

Front	Front was first published by Cabal Communications in 1998, it was created to rival IPC's publication Loaded, catering to a demographic of 16-25 year-old males. It began as part of the British "lads' mag" genre of magazines though the covers rejects this description with the statement "Front is no lads' mag". Whilst a major selling point is the photo-shoots of models, the magazine also focuses heavily on music, films, gadgets and games, plus sections on fashion and sport.
World	WORLD Magazine is a biweekly Christian news magazine, published in the United States of America by God's World Publications, a non-profit 501(c)(3) organization based in Asheville, North Carolina. WORLD differs from most other news magazines in that its declared perspective is one of conservative evangelical Protestantism. Its mission statement is "To report, interpret, and illustrate the news in a timely, accurate, enjoyable, and arresting fashion from a perspective committed to the Bible as the inerrant Word of God." Each issue features both U.S. and international news, cultural analysis, editorials and commentary, as well as book, music and movie reviews.
Ahmad	Ahmad and Ahmed are the principal transliterations of the Arabic given name . The latter name comes from the Arabic triconsonantal root of ?-M-D, meaning "highly praised", implying "one who constantly thanks Allah". Etymology One of the Islamic prophet Muhammad's many names is Ahmad, the name "Muhammad" pre-dating "Ahmad".
Shaykh Ahmad	Shaykh Ahmad ibn Zayn al-Dín ibn Ibráhím al-Ahsá'í was (1753 - 1826) was the founder of a 19th century Shi`i school in the Persian and Ottoman empires, whose followers are known as Shaykhís.

He was a native of the Al-Ahsa region, educated in Bahrain and the theological centers of Najaf and Karbala in Iraq. Spending the last twenty years of his life in Iran, he received the protection and patronage of princes of the Qajar dynasty.

Abdullah

Abdullah is a common Arabic male name. Humility before Allah is an essential value of Islam, hence Abdullah is a favorite name among Muslims. It was once common among Arabic-speaking Jews as well, especially Iraqi Jews.

Arab

The proper name Arab or "Arabian" (and cognates in other languages) has been used to translate several different but similar sounding words in ancient and classical texts which do not necessarily have the same meaning or origin. Grunebaum, in his book Classical Islam said that an approximate translation is "passerby" or "nomad". Will Durant, in The Age of Faith, said that Arab meant Arid.

Arabia

Arabia was a satrapy (province) of the Achaemenid Empire and later of the Sassanid Empire, by the name of Arabistan.

Achaemenid Era

Achaemenid Arabia corresponded to the lands between Egypt and Mesopotamia, known as Arabia Petraea. According to Herodotus, the Cambyses did not subdue the Arabs when he attacked Egypt in 525 BCE. His successor Darius the Great does not mention the Arabs in the Behistun inscription from the first years of his reign, but mentions them in later texts.

Ashkenazi Jews

Ashkenazi Jews, are the Jews descended from the medieval Jewish communities along the Rhine in Germany from Alsace in the south to the Rhineland in the north. Ashkenaz is the medieval Hebrew name for this region and thus for Germany. Thus, Ashkenazim or Ashkenazi Jews are literally "German Jews." Later, Jews from Western and Central Europe came to be called "Ashkenaz" because the main centers of Jewish learning were located in Germany.

Saudi Arabia

The Kingdom of Saudi Arabia, commonly known as Saudi Arabia is, in land area, the third largest Arab country and the largest country in the Middle East. It is bordered by Jordan and Iraq on the north and northeast, Kuwait, Qatar and the United Arab Emirates on the east, Oman on the southeast, and Yemen on the south. It is also connected to Bahrain by the King Fahd Causeway.

Arafat	Arafat is a surname or given name, and may refer to:
	<ul><li>Yasser Arafat</li><li>Fathi Arafat Palestinian physician</li><li>Moussa Arafat cousin of Yasser Arafat</li><li>Raed Arafat Romanian physician</li><li>Suha Arafat widow of Yasser Arafat</li><li>Yasir Arafat , Pakistani cricketer</li></ul>

Chapter 12. IMAGE VS. REALITY

Aqaba	Aqaba is a coastal town in the far south of Jordan. It is the capital of Aqaba Governorate. Aqaba is strategically important to Jordan as it is the country's only seaport.
Barak	Barak, Al-Buraq the son of Abinoam from Kedesh in Naphtali, was a military general in the Book of Judges in the Bible. He was the commander of the army of Deborah, the prophetess and heroine of the Hebrew Bible. Barak and Deborah are credited with defeating the Canaanite armies led by Sisera, who for twenty years had oppressed the Israelites.
Ehud	Ehud ben-Gera is described in the Biblical Book of Judges as a judge who was sent by God to deliver the Israelites from the Moabite yoke. Ehud was sent to the Moabite King Eglon on the pretext of delivering the Israelites' annual tribute. He had blacksmiths make a double-edged shortsword about eighteen inches long, useful for a stabbing thrust.
Hama	Hama is a city on the banks of the Orontes River in central Syria north of Damascus. It is the provincial capital of the Hama Governorate. The city is the location of the historical city Hamath.
Jerusalem	Jerusalem [ii] is the capital of Israel, though not internationally recognized as such.[iii] If the area and population of East Jerusalem is included, it is Israel's largest city in both population and area, with a population of 763,800 residents over an area of 125.1 km^2 (48.3 sq mi).[iv] Located in the Judean Mountains, between the Mediterranean Sea and the northern edge of the Dead Sea, modern Jerusalem has grown far beyond the boundaries of the Old City. Jerusalem is a holy city to the three major Abrahamic religions--Judaism, Christianity and Islam. In Judaism, Jerusalem has been the holiest city since, according to the Torah, King David of Israel first established it as the capital of the united Kingdom of Israel in c. 1000 BCE, and his son Solomon commissioned the building of the First Temple in the city.
Palestine	Palestine (Greek: Παλαιστ?νη, Palaistine; Latin: Palaestina; Hebrew: ????????? Eretz-Yisra'el, (formerly also ????????, Palestina); Arabic: ??????? Filas?in, Falas?in, Filis?in) is a conventional name used, among others, to describe a geographic region between the Mediterranean Sea and the Jordan River, and various adjoining lands.

Other terms for the same area include Canaan, Zion, the Land of Israel, and the Holy Land. Southern Levant is another purely geographic term, often implemented for the region, which does not have political or theologic implications.

Sharm el-Sheikh

Sharm el-Sheikh is a city situated on the southern tip of the Sinai Peninsula, in South Sinai Governorate, Egypt, on the coastal strip along the Red Sea with a population of approximately 35,000 (2008). Sharm el-Sheikh is the administrative hub of Egypt's South Sinai Governorate which includes the smaller coastal towns of Dahab and Nuweiba as well as the mountainous interior, Saint Catherine's Monastery and Mount Sinai.

Name

Sharm el-Sheikh is sometimes called the "City of Peace", referring to the large number of international peace conferences that have been held there.

State

The term state is used in various senses by Catholic theologians and spiritual writers.

It may be taken to signify a profession or calling in life, as where St. Paul says, in I Corinthians 7:20: "Let every man abide in the same calling in which he was called". States are classified in the Catholic Church as the clerical state, the religious state, and the secular state; and among religious states, again, we have those of the contemplative, the active, and the mixed orders.

World

WORLD Magazine is a biweekly Christian news magazine, published in the United States of America by God's World Publications, a non-profit 501(c)(3) organization based in Asheville, North Carolina. WORLD differs from most other news magazines in that its declared perspective is one of conservative evangelical Protestantism. Its mission statement is "To report, interpret, and illustrate the news in a timely, accurate, enjoyable, and arresting fashion from a perspective committed to the Bible as the inerrant Word of God."

Each issue features both U.S. and international news, cultural analysis, editorials and commentary, as well as book, music and movie reviews.

Zionism

Zionism is a Jewish political movement that, in its broadest sense, has supported the self-determination of the Jewish people in a sovereign Jewish national homeland. Since the establishment of the State of Israel, the Zionist movement continues primarily to advocate on behalf of the Jewish state and address threats to its continued existence and security. In a less common usage, the term may also refer to 1) non-political, Cultural Zionism, founded and represented most prominently by Ahad Ha'am; and 2) political support for the State of Israel by non-Jews, as in Christian Zionism.

Prime

Prime, is a fixed time of prayer of the traditional Divine Office (Canonical Hours), said at the first hour of daylight (approximately 6:00 a.m)., between the morning Hour of Lauds and the 9 a.m. Hour of Terce. It is part of the Christian liturgies of Eastern Christianity, but in the Latin Rite it was suppressed by the Second Vatican Council. However, clergy who have an obligation to celebrate the Liturgy of the Hours may still fulfil their obligation by using the Roman Breviary promulgated by Pope John XXIII in 1962, which contains the Hour of Prime.

Response

A response is the second half of one of a set of preces, the said or sung answer by the congregation or choir to a versicle said or sung by an officiant or cantor. In the following opening of the Anglican service of Evening Prayer according to the Book of Common Prayer (BCP), the first line is the versicle and the second is the response.

In some liturgical books (such as hymnals or breviaries) the symbol "R/" or "?" is used to denote a response.

Arab

The proper name Arab or "Arabian" (and cognates in other languages) has been used to translate several different but similar sounding words in ancient and classical texts which do not necessarily have the same meaning or origin. Grunebaum, in his book Classical Islam said that an approximate translation is "passerby" or "nomad". Will Durant, in The Age of Faith, said that Arab meant Arid.

CRamioi

Chapter 12. IMAGE VS. REALITY

Arafat	Arafat is a surname or given name, and may refer to: • Yasser Arafat • Fathi Arafat Palestinian physician • Moussa Arafat cousin of Yasser Arafat • Raed Arafat Romanian physician • Suha Arafat widow of Yasser Arafat • Yasir Arafat , Pakistani cricketer .
Hebron	Hebron, is located in the southern West Bank, 30 km (19 mi) south of Jerusalem. Nestled in the Judean Mountains, it lies 930 meters (3,050 ft) above sea level. It is the largest city in the West Bank and home to around 165,000 Palestinians, and over 500 Jewish settlers concentrated in and around the old quarter.
India	India was an ecclesiastical province of the Church of the East, at least nominally, from the seventh to the sixteenth century. The Malabar Coast of India had long been home to a thriving East Syrian (Nestorian) Christian community, known as the St. Thomas Christians. The community traces its origins to the evangelical activity of Thomas the Apostle in the 1st century.
Syria	Syria, officially the Syrian Arab Republic, is a country in Western Asia, bordering Lebanon and the Mediterranean Sea to the West, Turkey to the north, Iraq to the east, Jordan to the south, and Israel to the southwest. The name Syria formerly comprised the entire region of the Levant, while the modern state encompasses the site of several ancient kingdoms and empires, including the Eblan civilization of the third millennium BC. In the Islamic era, its capital city, Damascus, was the seat of the Umayyad Empire and a provincial capital of the Mamluk Empire. Damascus is one of the oldest continuously inhabited cities in the world.
Peace	Peace is an Athenian Old Comedy written and produced by the Greek playwright Aristophanes. It won second prize at the City Dionysia where it was staged just a few days before the ratification of the Peace of Nicias (421 BC), which promised to end the ten year old Peloponnesian War. The play is notable for its joyous anticipation of peace and for its celebration of a return to an idyllic life in the countryside.

Chapter 12. IMAGE VS. REALITY

Ariel	Ariel is an Israeli settlement and a city in the central West Bank. Established in 1978, its population at the end of 2009 was 17,600, including 7,000 immigrants who came to Israel after 1990. It is the fourth largest Jewish settlement city in the West Bank., after Modi'in Illit, Beitar Illit, and Ma'ale Adumim. In Hebrew, Ariel, literally means 'Lion of God'.
Cold War	Cold War is a video game developed by Czech developer Mindware Studios and published by DreamCatcher Games (Linux Game Publishing for Linux). The game is similar to the Splinter Cell series of games in that it uses a stealth-action system of gameplay. The game distinguishes itself by adding an invention system where the player can use seemingly useless objects to create tools and weapons.
Husayn	Husayn is an Arabic name which is the diminutive of Hassan, meaning "good", "handsome" or "beautiful". It is commonly given as a male given name among Muslims, in honor of Husayn ibn Ali (626-680 AD). In some Persian sources the forms ?osayn, Hosayn, or Hossein is used.
Front	Front was first published by Cabal Communications in 1998, it was created to rival IPC's publication Loaded, catering to a demographic of 16-25 year-old males. It began as part of the British "lads' mag" genre of magazines though the covers rejects this description with the statement "Front is no lads' mag". Whilst a major selling point is the photo-shoots of models, the magazine also focuses heavily on music, films, gadgets and games, plus sections on fashion and sport.
Hovevei Zion	Hovevei Zion, refers to organizations that are now considered the forerunners and foundation-builders of modern Zionism.

Many of these first groups were established in Eastern European countries in the early 1880s with the aim to promote Jewish immigration to the Land of Israel, then a part of Ottoman Empire, and advance Jewish settlement there, particularly agricultural. Most of them stayed away from politics.

Israeli settlement

An Israeli settlement is an Israeli civilian community on land that was captured by Israel during the Six-Day War and is considered by the international community (excluding Israel) to be occupied territory. Such settlements currently exist in the West Bank, East Jerusalem, and the Golan Heights.

The International Court of Justice and the international community say these settlements are illegal,.

East Jerusalem

East Jerusalem refers to the parts of Jerusalem captured by Jordan in the 1948 Arab-Israeli War and then taken by Israel in the 1967 Six-Day War. It includes Jerusalem's Old City and some of the holiest sites of Judaism, Christianity, and Islam, such as the Temple Mount, Western Wall, Al-Aqsa Mosque, and the Church of the Holy Sepulchre. The term "East Jerusalem" may refer to either the area under Jordanian rule between 1949 and 1967 which was incorporated into the municipality of Jerusalem after 1967, covering some 70 km^2 (27 sq mi), or the territory of the pre-1967 Jordanian municipality, covering 6.4 km^2 (2.5 sq mi).

Old City

The Old City is a 0.9 square kilometer (0.35 square mile) walled area within the modern city of Jerusalem. Until the 1860s this area constituted the entire city of Jerusalem. The Old City is home to several sites of key religious importance: the Temple Mount and its Western Wall for Jews, the Church of the Holy Sepulchre for Christians, and the Dome of the Rock and al-Aqsa Mosque for Muslims.

Temple

In the Latter Day Saint movement, a temple is a building dedicated to be a house of God and is reserved for special forms of worship. A temple differs from a church meetinghouse, which is used for weekly worship services. Temples have been a significant part of the Latter Day Saint movement since early in its inception.

323

Chapter 12. IMAGE VS. REALITY

Temple Mount	The Temple Mount, also known in the Bible as Mount Moriah (some also identify it with the biblical Mount Zion) and by Muslims as the Noble Sanctuary (Bait-ul-Muqaddas), is a religious site in the Old City of Jerusalem. Judaism regards the Temple Mount as the place where God chose the Divine Presence to rest (Isa 8:18); it was from here the world expanded into its present form and where God gathered the dust used to create the first man, Adam.{According to the sages of the Talmud[13]} The site is the location of Abraham's binding of Isaac, and of two Jewish Temples. According to the Bible the site should function as the center of all national life - government, judicial and, of course, religious center (Deut 12:5-26; 14:23-25; 15:20; 16:2-16; 17:8-10; 26: 2; 31: 11; Isa 2: 2-5; Oba 1:21; Psa 48) .
West Bank	The West Bank of the Jordan River is the landlocked geographical eastern part of the Palestinian territories located in the Western Asia. To the west, north, and south, the West Bank shares borders with the state of Israel. To the east, across the Jordan River, lies the Hashemite Kingdom of Jordan.
Impact	Impact is a monthly magazine published in the United Kingdom. It covers the field of action entertainment: including Hong Kong action cinema, worldwide martial arts films, Hollywood productions, anime, comics, action films and East Asian cinema in general. Originally founded and edited by Bey Logan, it is presently edited by John Mosby, with Mike Leeder acting as Eastern Editor from the Hong Kong office, and Andrez Bergen as Tokyo Correspondent.
Emir	Emir, ("commander" or "general", also "prince" ; also transliterated as amir, aamir or ameer) is a high title of nobility or office, used throughout the Muslim world. Emirs are usually considered high-ranking sheikhs, but in monarchical states the term is also used for princes, with "Emirate" being analogous to principality in this sense. While emir is the predominant spelling in English and many other languages, amir, closer to the original Arabic, is more common for its numerous compounds (e.g. admiral) and in individual names.

Chapter 12. IMAGE VS. REALITY

Arab nationalism	Arab nationalism is a nationalist ideology celebrating the glories of Arab civilization, the language and literature of the Arabs, calling for rejuvenation and political union in the Arab world. Its central premise is that the peoples of the Arab World, from the Atlantic Ocean to the Arabian Sea, constitute one nation bound together by common linguistic, cultural, religious, and historical heritage, One of the primary goals of Arab nationalism is the end of Western influence in the Arab World, seen as a "nemesis" of Arab strength, and the removal of those Arab governments considered to be dependent upon Western power. It rose to prominence with the weakening and defeat of the Ottoman Empire in the early 20th century and declined after the defeat of the Arab armies in the Six Day War.
Christian	A Christian is a person who adheres to Christianity, an Abrahamic, monotheistic religion based on the life and teachings of Jesus of Nazareth as recorded in the Canonical gospels and the letters of the New Testament. Central to the Christian faith is love or Agape. Christians also believe Jesus is the Messiah prophesied in the Hebrew Bible, the Son of God, and the savior of mankind from their sins.
Egypt	The Roman province of Egypt was established in 30 BC after Octavian (the future emperor Augustus) defeated his rival Mark Antony, deposed his lover Queen Cleopatra VII and annexed the Ptolemaic kingdom of Egypt to the Roman Empire. The province encompassed most of modern-day Egypt except for the Sinai Peninsula (which would later be conquered by Trajan). Aegyptus was bordered by the provinces of Creta et Cyrenaica to the West and Judaea to the East.
Revisionist Zionism	Revisionist Zionism is a nationalist faction within the Zionist movement. It is the founding ideology of the non-religious right in Israel, and was the chief ideological competitor to the dominant socialist Labor Zionism. Revisionism is represented primarily by the Likud Party.
Libya	Libya was a satrapy of the Achaemenid Empire according to King Darius I of Persia Naqshe Rustam and King Xerxes I of Persia' Daiva inscription. It is also mentioned as being part of the 6th district by Herodotus, which also included Cyrene, a Greek colony in Libya. When King Cambyses II of Persia conquered Egypt, the king of Cyrene, Arcesilaus III, sided with Persia.
Allies	Allies is a Christian rock band. They released six albums during the 1980s and early 1990s. Band members

Chapter 12. IMAGE VS. REALITY

The most notable band members were guitarist Randy Thomas, formerly of the Jesus music group Sweet Comfort Band and vocalist Bob Carlisle.

Emunim	Emunim is a moshav in central Israel. Located near Ashdod, it falls under the jurisdiction of Be'er Tuvia Regional Council. In 2006 it had a population of 732

The moshav was founded in 1950 by immigrants from Egypt, on the land of the Palestinian village of Beit Daras.

Irgun

Irgun was a Zionist paramilitary group that operated in the British mandate of Palestine between 1931 and 1948. It was an offshoot of the earlier and larger Jewish paramilitary organization Haganah . Since the group originally broke from the Haganah it became known as the Haganah Bet, or alternatively as Haganah Ha'leumit (????? ???????) or Ha'ma'amad (??????). Irgun members were absorbed into the Israel Defence Forces at the start of the 1948 Arab-Israeli war.

Vladimir

Vladimir is a male Slavic given name of Church Slavonic and Old East Slavic origin, now widespread throughout all Slavic nations. It is also a common name in former Soviet non-Slavic countries where Christianity is practiced, such as Armenia.

Max Vasmer in his Etymological Dictionary of Russian Language explains the name as meaning "regal".

Western

Western is a Franco-Belgian one shot comic written by Jean Van Hamme, illustrated by Grzegorz Rosinski and published by Le Lombard in French and Cinebook in English.

Story

Volume

329

Chapter 12. IMAGE VS. REALITY

- Western - May 2001 ISBN 2-80361-662-9

Translations

Cinebook Ltd plans to publish Western in June 2011

Definitions

Definitions is a dictionary of about 185 philosophical terms sometimes included in the corpus of Plato's works. Plato is generally not regarded as the editor of all of Definitions. Some ancient scholars attributed Definitions to Speusippus.

Judea

35°18′23″E? / ?31.69889°N 35.30639°E

Judea, when Roman Judea was renamed Syria Palaestina following the Jewish Bar Kokhba revolt.

Etymology

The name Judea is a Greek and Roman adaptation of the name "Judah", which originally encompassed the territory of the Israelite tribe of that name and later of the ancient Kingdom of Judah. It was the name in use in English throughout history until the Jordanian occupation of the area.

Samaria

Samaria is a term used for a mountainous region roughly corresponding to the northern part of the West Bank. According to 1 Kings 16:24, it is derived from the individual [or clan] Shemer, from whom Omri purchased the site. The name was the only name used for this area from ancient times until the Jordanian conquest of 1948, at which point the Jordanian occupiers coined the term West Bank.

Chapter 12. IMAGE VS. REALITY

Barghouti

Barghouti is the last name of a prominent Palestinian family. Many members are involved in Palestinian politics and come from Ramallah's most prominent towns Aboud, Deir Ghassanah, Kobar and Bani Zeid.

List of notable members

- Abdullatif Barghouti was a poet and a writer who specialized in Palestinian Folklore.
- Bashir Barghouti Palestinian Communist and journalist
- Hussein Barghouti was a poet and writer.
- Marwan Barghouti is a leader of Fatah, the military branch of the Palestinian Authority and the Palestine Liberation Organization and convicted murderer for actions during the Second Intifada.
- Mohammad Barghouti, former Labour Minister of the Palestinian Authority.
- Mourid Barghouti is a poet and a writer.
- Mustafa Barghouti is a medical doctor, Palestinian democracy activist, founder of the Union of Palestinian Medical Relief Committees, and advocate of non-violent resistance to Israeli occupation.
- Omar Barghouti is an independent Palestinian political analyst.
- Tamim Al Barghouti poet and political scientist, son of Mourid Barghouti

Chapter 12. IMAGE VS. REALITY

Chapter 12. IMAGE VS. REALITY

| Marwan | Marwan is an Arabic male name. It may refer to: |

Given name

- Abu Marwan Abd al-Malik I Saadi, King of Morocco (1576-1578)
- Marwan I, Umayyad caliph (623-685)
- Marwan II, Umayyad caliph (688-750)
- Marwan Ali, Tunisian pop singer
- Marwan Barghouti, leader of the Palestinian group Fatah
- Marwan Hamadeh, Lebanese politician
- Marwan Hamed, Egyptian film director
- Marwan Khoury, Lebanese artist
- Marwan al-Muasher, Jordanian politician
- Marwan al-Shehhi, Emirati hijacker-pilot who crashed United Airlines Flight 175 into the second World Trade Center tower

Surname

- Ashraf Marwan, Egyptian businessman
- Asma bint Marwan, a medieval Arabian female poet (7th century)
- Ibn Marwan, chieftain in the Al-Andalus (9th century)
- Ubayd Allah Abu Marwan, general in the Al-Andalus (8th/9th century)

Fictional characters

- Habib Marwan, character in the TV drama 24

Other uses

- Marwanid (990-1085), Kurdish dynasty

.

Abdullah

Abdullah is a common Arabic male name. Humility before Allah is an essential value of Islam, hence Abdullah is a favorite name among Muslims. It was once common among Arabic-speaking Jews as well, especially Iraqi Jews.

ClamIoI

Chapter 12. IMAGE VS. REALITY

Henry	Henry is an English male given name and a surname, from the Old French Henry derived itself from the Germanic name Haimric, which was derived from the word elements haim, meaning "home" and ric, meaning "power, ruler". Harry, its English short form, was considered the "spoken form" of Henry in medieval England. Most English kings named Henry were called Harry.
Transjordan	The Transjordan is a section of the land of Israel mentioned in the Hebrew Bible. It is the land east of the Jordan River in which the tribes of Reuben and Gad, and half the tribe of Manasseh settle.

Name

The prefix trans- is Latin and means "across" or beyond, and so "Transjordan" refers to the land on the other side of the Jordan River. |
| Lebanon | Lebanon is a mural size painting by Nabil Kanso depicting the Lebanese Civil War in a scene invoking the spirit and character of the people in the midst of horror and violence gripping the country. Amid the scene of chaos and devastation, two central figures reach across toward each other symbolically to represent the appeal for unity in defiance of the forces of division, destruction, and terror.

Description

Painted in oil on linen and completed in 1983, the painting Lebanon measures 28 feet (8.5 meters) long by 10 feet (3meters) tall. |
| Al-Islah | Al-Islah, is a political party in Yemen that is absent from the Yemeni parliament. According to Al Jazeera, its ideology is partly based on Islamism. One of its main leaders is Tawakel Karman, who is also a member of parliament for the similarly named Al-Islah party that has 46 parliamentary seats. |

Chapter 12. IMAGE VS. REALITY

Damascus	Damascus is the capital and the second largest city of Syria as well as one of the country's 14 governorates. The Damascus Governorate is ruled by a governor appointed by the Minister of Interior. In addition to being the oldest continuously inhabited city in the world, Damascus is a major cultural and religious center of the Levant.
Arab Revolt	The Arab Revolt was initiated by the Sherif Hussein bin Ali with the aim of securing independence from the ruling Ottoman Turks and creating a single unified Arab state spanning from Aleppo in Syria to Aden in Yemen. The rise of nationalism under the Ottoman Empire goes back to 1821. Arab nationalism has its roots in the Mashriq, particularly in countries of Sham (the Levant). The political orientation of Arab nationalists in the years prior to the Great War was generally moderate.
Arabia	Arabia was a satrapy (province) of the Achaemenid Empire and later of the Sassanid Empire, by the name of Arabistan. Achaemenid Era Achaemenid Arabia corresponded to the lands between Egypt and Mesopotamia, known as Arabia Petraea. According to Herodotus, the Cambyses did not subdue the Arabs when he attacked Egypt in 525 BCE. His successor Darius the Great does not mention the Arabs in the Behistun inscription from the first years of his reign, but mentions them in later texts.
Saudi Arabia	The Kingdom of Saudi Arabia, commonly known as Saudi Arabia is, in land area, the third largest Arab country and the largest country in the Middle East. It is bordered by Jordan and Iraq on the north and northeast, Kuwait, Qatar and the United Arab Emirates on the east, Oman on the southeast, and Yemen on the south. It is also connected to Bahrain by the King Fahd Causeway.
Paris	Paris, the son of Priam, king of Troy, appears in a number of Greek legends. Probably the best-known was his elopement with Helen, queen of Sparta, this being one of the immediate causes of the Trojan War. Later in the war, he fatally wounds Achilles in the heel with an arrow, as foretold by Achilles's mother, Thetis.

Chapter 12. IMAGE VS. REALITY

San Remo conference	The San Remo Conference was an international meeting of the post-World War I Allied Supreme Council, held in Sanremo, Italy, from 19 to 26 April 1920. It was attended by the four Principal Allied Powers of World War I who were represented by the prime ministers of Britain (David Lloyd George), France (Alexandre Millerand) and Italy (Francesco Nitti) and by Japan's Ambassador K. Matsui.
	It determined the allocation of Class "A" League of Nations mandates for administration of the former Ottoman-ruled lands of the Middle East.
	The precise boundaries of all territories were left unspecified, to "be determined by the Principal Allied Powers" and were not finalized until four years later.
Western Wall	The Western Wall, Wailing Wall or Kotel ; is located in the Old City of Jerusalem at the foot of the western side of the Temple Mount. It is a remnant of the ancient wall that surrounded the Jewish Temple's courtyard and is one of the most sacred sites in Judaism outside of the Temple Mount itself. Just over half the wall, including its 17 courses located below street level, dates from the end of the Second Temple period, being constructed around 19 BCE by Herod the Great.
Alexander	Alexander, son of Perseus of Macedon, was a child at the conquest of his father by the Romans, and after the triumph of Aemilus Paullus in 167 BC, was kept in custody at Alba Fucens, together with his father. He became skilful in the toreutic art, learned the Latin language, and became a public notary.
Correspondence	In theology, correspondence is the relationship between spiritual and natural realities, or between mental and physical realities. The term was coined by the 18th century theologian Emanuel Swedenborg in his Arcana Coelestia (1749-1756) and Heaven and Hell (1758) and other works.
	Swedenborg states that there is a correspondence between, for example: thought and speech, between intention and action, between mind and body, and between God and creation.

341

Chapter 12. IMAGE VS. REALITY

Baghdad	Baghdad is the capital of Iraq, as well as the coterminous Baghdad Governorate. With an estimated population between 7 and 7.5 million, it is the largest city in Iraq, the second largest city in the Arab World (after Cairo, Egypt), and the second largest city in Western Asia (after Tehran, Iran). Located along the Tigris River, the city was founded in the 8th century and became the capital of the Abbasid Caliphate.
Kuwait	The State of Kuwait is a sovereign Arab nation situated in the northeast of the Arabian Peninsula in Western Asia. It is bordered by Saudi Arabia to the south, and Iraq to the north. It lies on the northwestern shore of the Persian Gulf.
Nuri	Nuri is a place in modern Sudan on the south (east) side of the Nile. Close to it, there are pyramids belonging to Nubian kings. Nuri is situated about 15 km north of Sanam, and 10 km from Jebel Barkal.
Ahmad	Ahmad and Ahmed are the principal transliterations of the Arabic given name . The latter name comes from the Arabic triconsonantal root of ?-M-D, meaning "highly praised", implying "one who constantly thanks Allah". Etymology One of the Islamic prophet Muhammad's many names is Ahmad, the name "Muhammad" pre-dating "Ahmad".
Sharif	Sharif or Chérif is a traditional Arab tribal title given to those who serve as the protector of the tribe and all tribal assets, such as property, wells, and land. In origin, the word is an adjective meaning "noble", "highborn". The feminine singular is sharifa(h) (.
Suez Crisis	The Suez Crisis, also referred to as the Tripartite Aggression, was a war fought by Britain, France, and Israel against Egypt beginning on 29 October 1956.

Chapter 12. IMAGE VS. REALITY

The attack followed Egypt's decision of 26 July 1956 to nationalize the Suez Canal, after the withdrawal of an offer by Britain and the United States to fund the building of the Aswan Dam, which was partly in response to Egypt recognizing the People's Republic of China during the height of tensions between China and Taiwan. Britain and France were also strongly opposed to Nasser's plan to annex the Sudan.

Camp David Accords

The Camp David Accords were signed by Egyptian President Anwar El Sadat and Israeli Prime Minister Menachem Begin on September 17, 1978, following thirteen days of secret negotiations at Camp David. The two framework agreements were signed at the White House, and were witnessed by United States President Jimmy Carter. The second of these frameworks, A Framework for the Conclusion of a Peace Treaty between Egypt and Israel, led directly to the 1979 Egypt-Israel Peace Treaty, and resulted in Sadat and Begin sharing the 1978 Nobel Peace Prize.

Politics

Aristotle's Politics is a work of political philosophy. The end of the Nicomachean Ethics declared that the inquiry into ethics necessarily follows into politics, and the two works are frequently considered to be parts of a larger treatise, or perhaps connected lectures, dealing with the "philosophy of human affairs." The title of the Politics literally means "the things concerning the polis."

Composition

The literary character of the Politics is subject to some dispute, growing out of the textual difficulties that attended the loss of Aristotle's works. Book III ends with a sentence that is repeated almost verbatim at the start of Book VII, while the intervening Books IV-VI seem to have a very different flavor from the rest; Book IV seems to refer several times back to the discussion of the best regime contained in Books VII-VIII. Some editors have therefore inserted Books VII-VIII after Book III. At the same time, however, references to the "discourses on politics" that occur in the Nicomachean Ethics suggest that the treatise as a whole ought to conclude with the discussion of education that occurs in Book VIII of the Politics, although it is not certain that Aristotle is referring to the Politics here.

| Labor Zionism | Labor Zionism can be described as the major stream of the left wing of the Zionist movement. It was, for many years, the most significant tendency among Zionists and Zionist organizational structure. It saw itself as the Zionist sector of the historic Jewish labor movements of Eastern and Central Europe, eventually developing local units in most countries with sizeable Jewish populations. |

Go to **Cram101.com** for Interactive Practice Exams for this book or virtually any of your books.
And, **NEVER** highlight a book again!

CPSIA information can be obtained at www.ICGtesting.com
Printed in the USA
BVOW06s1117050814

361738BV00005B/328/P